Studies in Matthew

The King and the Kingdom

Studies in

MATTHEW

THE KING
AND THE KINGDOM

Roland Q. Leavell

Convention Press

NASHVILLE   TENNESSEE

Code Number: Church Study Course
This book is number 0226 in category 2, section
for Adults and Young People.

Library of Congress Catalog Card Number: 62–10285
Printed in the United States of America
392. JUL 62 R.R.D.

About the Author

ROLAND QUINCHE LEAVELL received the B.A. and M.A. degrees from the University of Mississippi in 1914. He received the Th.M. degree from Southern Baptist Theological Seminary in 1917, and the Th.D. from the same seminary in 1925. In 1937 Mercer University conferred on him the D.D. degree, and in 1945 John B. Stetson University honored him with the LL.D. degree.

Dr. Leavell was professor of mathematics in Oxford, Mississippi, high school, 1911-13. He was ordained to the Baptist ministry December 28, 1913. During World War I, he served as overseas YMCA secretary, 1917-19. He was pastor of the First Baptist Church, Oxford, Mississippi, 1919-23; of First Baptist Church, Picayune, Mississippi, 1925-27; of First Baptist Church, Gainesville, Georgia, 1927-36; and of First Baptist Church, Tampa, Florida, 1942-46.

He has held various positions in the Southern Baptist Convention and in state conventions. He was Mississippi representative for the Foreign Mission Board, 1927; Georgia representative for the Home Mission Board, 1929-36; vice-president of the Georgia Baptist Convention, 1929-30; superintendent of evangelism, Home Mission Board, 1937-42; secretary, Committee on Evangelism, Baptist World Alliance, 1939-57; chairman, Commission on Evangelism, Baptist World Alliance, 1957-60; vice-president, Mississippi Baptist Convention, 1958-59 and vice-president of the Southern Baptist Convention, 1961-62. From 1946-58 he was president of New Orleans Baptist Seminary, and since 1958 he has been president emeritus.

In 1920 Dr. Leavell toured Southern Baptist mission fields in China and Japan. He toured mission fields in the Holy Land, 1934 and 1955 and in Europe, 1937, 1947, 1949, and 1955. He was a member of the Foreign Mission Board preaching mission to Japan in 1951 and visiting lecturer to South American Baptist theological seminaries in 1953.

His wife is Lilian Yarborough Leavell. They have three daughters: Mrs. Wesley (Mary D.) Bowman, Alexandria, Louisiana;

Mrs. Maynard (Lilian) Fountain, New Orleans, Louisiana; Mrs. Carl (Dorothea) Hudson, Bunkie, Louisiana; and eight grandchildren.

Dr. Leavell's writings include *Landrum Pinson Leavell, an Unashamed Workman*, 1932; *Winning Others to Christ*, 1936; *Helping Others to Become Christians*, 1938; *Saving America to Save the World*, 1940; *The Romance of Evangelism*, 1943; *Christianity Our Citadel*, 1943; *Evangelism, Christ's Imperative Commission*, 1951; *Corra Berry Leavell, Christian Mother*, 1952. He was editor and compiler of *Preaching the Doctrines of Grace*, 1939. He has contributed to the *Encyclopedia of Southern Baptists* and denominational journals.

He is listed in *Who's Who in America*, 1960-61.

Contents

Church Study Course

THE CHURCH STUDY COURSE began October 1, 1959. It is a merger of three courses previously promoted by the Sunday School Board—the Sunday School Training Course, the Graded Training Union Study Course, and the Church Music Training Course. On October 1, 1961, the Woman's Missionary Union principles and methods studies were added.

The course is fully graded. The system of awards provides a series of five diplomas of twenty books each for Adults or Young People, two diplomas of five books each for Intermediates, and two diplomas of five books each for Juniors. Book awards earned previously in the Sunday School Training Course, the Graded Training Union Study Course, and the Church Music Training Course may be transferred to the new course.

The course is comprehensive, with books grouped into twenty categories. The purpose of the course is to help Christians to grow in knowledge and conviction, to help them to grow toward maturity in Christian character and competence for service, to encourage them to participate worthily as workers in their churches, and to develop leaders for all phases of church life and work.

The Church Study Course is promoted by the Baptist Sunday School Board, 127 Ninth Avenue, North, Nashville, Tennessee, through its Sunday School, Training Union, Church Music, and Church Administration departments; by the Woman's Missionary Union, 600 North Twentieth Street, Birmingham, Alabama; and by the respective departments in the states affiliated with the Southern Baptist Convention. A description of the course and the system of awards may be found in the leaflet, "Trained Workmen," which may be obtained without charge from any one of these departments.

A record of all awards earned should be maintained in each church. A person should be designated by the church to keep the files. Forms for such records may be ordered from any Baptist Book Store.

Requirements for Credit in Class or Home Study

IF CREDIT is desired for the study of this book in a class or by home study, the following requirements must be met:

I. IN CLASSWORK

1. The class must meet a minimum of seven and one-half clock hours. The required time does not include assembly periods. Ten class periods of forty-five minutes each are recommended. (If laboratory or clinical work is desired in specialized or technical courses, this requirement may be met by six clock hours of classwork and three clock hours of supervised laboratory or clinical work.)

2. A class member who attends all class sessions and completes the reading of the book within a week following the last class session will not be required to do any written work for credit.

3. A class member who is absent from one or more sessions must answer the questions (pp. 145–146) on all chapters he misses. In such a case, he must turn in his paper within a week, and he must certify that he has read the book.

4. The teacher should request an award for himself. A person who teaches a book in the section for Intermediates or Juniors (any category) or conducts an approved unit of instruction for Nursery, Beginner, or Primary children will be granted an award in category 11, Special Studies, which will count as an elective on his own diploma. He should specify in his request the name of the book taught or the unit conducted for Nursery, Beginner, or Primary children.

5. The teacher should complete the "Request for Book Awards —Class Study" (Form 150) and forward it within two weeks after the completion of the class to the Church Study Course Awards Office, 127 Ninth Avenue, North, Nashville 3, Tennessee.

II. IN HOME STUDY

1. A person who does not attend any class session may receive

credit by answering all questions for written work as indicated in the book (pp. 145–146). When a person turns in his paper on home study, he must certify that he has read the book.

2. Students may find profit in studying the text together, but individual papers are required. Carbon copies or duplicates in any form cannot be accepted.

3. Home study work papers may be graded by the pastor or a person designated by him, or they may be sent to the Church Study Course Awards Office for grading. The form entitled "Request for Book Awards—Home Study" (Form 151) must be used in requesting awards. It should be mailed to Church Study Course Awards Office, 127 Ninth Avenue, North, Nashville 3, Tennessee.

III. CREDIT FOR THIS BOOK

This book is number 0226 in category 2, section for Adults and Young People.

CHAPTER 1

1

Introduction

THE CENTRAL THEME of the Gospel of Matthew is the most magnificent subject in heaven or upon earth, the kingdom of heaven. That was the "magnificent obsession" of Christ. The Gospel is one of the noblest books in any literature, either sacred or secular. It is scholarly written, topically arranged, logically developed, and triumphantly concluded. Although it was written after Mark's Gospel, Matthew's story soon took first place in all groupings of the four Gospels and was fixed there in the canon of the New Testament.

I. THE AUTHOR

Although there is no statement in the first Gospel to tell who wrote it, there are good reasons for believing that the book was written by Matthew—sometimes called Levi—the son of Alphaeus, the tax collector, who became one of the twelve apostles (Matt. 9:9). Early Christian writers and Christian tradition attribute the Gospel to this Matthew.

Matthew was an ideal man to record the teachings of Jesus for his own and succeeding generations to read. He was a man of letters and linguistic abilities, since as a tax collector undoubtedly he knew both the Aramaic and the Greek languages. Tax collectors were men of figures and note-taking and details; many were proficient in the use of shorthand. Such skills are indicated in Matthew's writing.

It is generally accepted that Mark wrote what Peter had told him about Jesus' works, but Mark tells little about Jesus' discourses. What would have been more natural than for

1

Matthew to read Mark's account of the activities of Jesus as Peter told them, and to feel that the great teachings as well as the deeds of Jesus should be known? Therefore, Matthew wrote a Greek manuscript relating many of Mark's accounts of the doings of Jesus, and he added his own accounts of the sayings of Jesus.

Papias of Hierapolis (died about A.D. 155) is quoted as having said that Matthew noted the sayings in the Aramaic language, and that others translated them. However, if Matthew did make notes in Aramaic, he himself was well qualified to translate them into Greek.

No other individual of the first century has ever been named as the author of the first Gospel. The book bears every evidence of authenticity and inspiration. It is evident that the writer had comprehended the great central message of Jesus, the kingdom of heaven, as only one who had sat under the compelling words of the Master could have done and that he felt compelled to give this message to the reading world.

II. THE DATE

The date of the Gospel of Matthew is usually judged to have been about the time of the persecutions by Nero (A.D. 64–68) or just after the destruction of Jerusalem by Titus (A.D. 70). Probably it was written early in the decade of A.D. 70–80.

III. CONTENT AND PURPOSE

Matthew's Gospel is the world's noblest treatise or thesis on the subject of Jesus, the King of the kingdom of heaven. It contains six great discourses and many parables about the kingdom that Mark does not give.

Matthew saw what a tragedy it would be for men not to have the truth about the birth of Jesus, the Sermon on the

Mount, the commission of the twelve, the parables explaining the kingdom, the denunciation of the hypocrisy of those Pharisees who opposed Jesus, the teachings about the destruction of Jerusalem, and the prophecies about Christ's second coming and the last judgment. It would have been a tragedy indeed for the Christian world not to have learned of the Great Commission as given in Matthew 28: 18–20.

Every word of Matthew is directly or indirectly related to an exposition of the truth about the King and the kingdom. The material is arranged topically, not chronologically.

Matthew pictures Jesus as one who was born a king, who lived like a king, who spoke like a king, who died like a king, who rose from the dead and promised to come again as the King of kings. As a king with regal authority, he stood upon the pinnacle of his resurrection glory and commanded his kingdom-minded followers to make disciples of all nations. His command is the divine imperative to every disciple of the King, until "the kingdom of the world is become the kingdom of our Lord, and of his Christ: and he shall reign for ever and ever" (Rev. 11:15, ASV).

IV. HISTORICAL BACKGROUND

To appreciate the situation in Judaism portrayed in the Gospels, one must recognize the changes which had taken place during the long interval of history which followed the restoration of the Temple and the city of Jerusalem under Zerubbabel, Ezra, and Nehemiah. Regarding this period, Dr. P. E. Burroughs wrote:

Between the two Testaments is an interval of about 400 years. From secular sources we know that the Jews exchanged rulers frequently during this period.

1. They remained under the Persian rule until the rise of Alexander the Great, 331 B.C.

2. They were ruled by the Greek kings from 331 to 167 B.C. In this period the Greek language became widely used among the Jews, resulting in the Septuagint translation of the Scriptures, a translation from the original Hebrew into Greek.

3. In 167 B.C., angered and outraged by the persecutions of Antiochus Epiphanes, the Jews threw off the foreign yoke, and for a hundred years they were independent.

4. In 63 B.C., Pompey conquered Jerusalem, and the Jewish people came under the Roman rule. In 37 B.C., Herod the Great became king, and continued until after the birth of Christ.

5. During this period the Jews underwent many changes and suffered much. Their language, their laws, their customs were changed so that in the days of our Lord we come upon conditions widely different from those which prevailed when Malachi wrote his prophecy.[1]

Zealously and tenaciously the Jewish people held to their sacred Scriptures. We are accustomed to being reminded of the encrustations of tradition and oral law which in time were added to the revealed Word of God. However, we must not lose sight of the loyal devotion to their religion which caused the Jews to preserve for us the Old Testament as we know it. We can never fully estimate our debt to the rabbis—even to the very scribes and Pharisees whom we condemn so glibly. The denunciations of Jesus upon these leaders were not because they were ungodly, but because, having such a rich religious heritage, they failed to measure up to what God expected of them.

FOR RESEARCH AND DISCUSSION

1. How does the Gospel of Matthew rank in importance to the Christian enterprise in comparison with the other Gospels?
2. Consult a good Bible handbook and determine what is the theme of each of the four Gospels?

---

[1] *Outlines of Bible History* (Nashville: Convention Press), p. 66. Out of print.

3. From a good encyclopedia, seek to learn how the canon of the New Testament took final shape.
4. Why did Matthew think it was so important for Christians to know the principles of the kingdom of heaven?

TO GUIDE YOUR SCRIPTURE READING

In this textbook Matthew's Gospel is outlined in seven parts. In your preparation for this study, read the entire Gospel, following the thought units indicated in the outline. As each section is approached during the study, reread it as a preparation for the class discussion.

1. The King Comes to Establish the Kingdom (1–4)
    Events leading up to the launching of the kingdom movement—the ancestry, birth, preparation, inauguration, and testing of the King
2. The Way of Life in the Kingdom (5–7)
    Statement of principles by which citizens of the kingdom are to live
3. The King Demonstrates His Power but Is Rejected (8–12)
    His power demonstrated over sickness, personal affairs, nature, demons, sin, social customs, religious ceremonies, death; his power delegated to his disciples; his power doubted, blasphemed, misunderstood
4. The King Explains the Kingdom and Announces His Program (13–16)
    The kingdom explained through parables and in the training of the twelve; program involves the establishment of the church, the plan of redemption, the dedication of disciples
5. The King Teaches Social and Spiritual Principles (17–20)
    The way of glorification; principles of victorious living, social relationships, true greatness
6. The King Claims Kingship and Is Again Rejected (21–25)
    Formal claims met by efforts to ensnare the King; predictions of woes and destruction, but also of final victory
7. The King Suffers a Cross to Win a Crown (26–28)
    Through betrayal and death to resurrection triumph; disciples commissioned to an ongoing program

CHAPTER 2

2

The Kingdom of Heaven

EVERY prophet, crusader, or world religious leader has had one dominant dedication which controlled his endeavors. With Buddha it was renunciation; with Confucius it was social righteousness; with Mohammed it was monotheism.

Christ's ultimate and all-inclusive purpose was and is to establish his kingdom—the reign of heaven in the hearts of men. This purpose he came to declare and to accomplish by giving his life for men. To redeem men and bring them into his kingdom was indeed his "magnificent obsession."

I. THE CONCEPT OF THE KINGDOM

Jesus offered, and is still offering, salvation, abundant life, and eternal glory to all who will accept his kingly rule. He is gloriously fulfilling his promise. The Gospel of Matthew is the divinely inspired manifesto concerning Jesus' heavenly rule in the hearts of men.

The word "kingdom" is a translation of the Greek word *basileia* (rule, or reign). It is found over one hundred and fifty times in the New Testament, and more than fifty times in Matthew. It is Matthew's characteristic word for the mission of Christ. The kingdom is not a kingdom *in* heaven, but a kingdom *of* heaven's rule in men.

No essential difference can be established between the kingdom of God and the kingdom of heaven. For example, Matthew used the term "kingdom of heaven" in relating the parable of the mustard seed (13:31) while Mark used "kingdom of God" in the same parable (4:30–31). "Kingdom of heaven" is used exclusively by Matthew; "kingdom of God" is used by the other New Testament writers and only a few times by Matthew.

Matthew was writing first of all to Jewish readers of his day, many of whom thought that God was exclusively the God of the Chosen People. They were inclined to interpret the term, "kingdom of God," as an exclusive blessing for Jewish people. Furthermore, since the Jews refrained from pronouncing the name of God, *Yahweh,* for fear of breaking the Third Commandment, they would tend to say "kingdom of heaven." The other New Testament writers were addressing not only Jews but also Gentiles who had formerly been idol worshipers. To impress their readers with the concept of the true God, they used the term "kingdom of God."

The kingdom concept was born in the minds of the Jews through their hopes for the coming of the Messiah. Through the prophet Nathan, God said to King David: "I will set up thy seed after thee, . . . and I will establish his kingdom. . . . I will stablish the throne of his kingdom for ever" (2 Sam. 7: 12–13). Psalm 2, a messianic psalm, says: "Ask of me, and I shall give thee the heathen for thine inheritance, and the uttermost parts of the earth for thy possession" (v. 8). Chapters 2, 9, and 11 in Isaiah tell in exalted terms of peace and prosperity under the powerful rule of the messianic king.

Many other psalms and many of the later prophets—for example, Ezekiel (34:24), Daniel (7:14), and Zechariah (9:9)—strengthened this hope in the hearts of Israel. The angel promised the virgin Mary that her Son should have "the throne of his father David," that he should "reign over the house of Jacob for ever," and that "of his kingdom there shall be no end" (Luke 1: 32–33).

II. THE KING OF THE KINGDOM

Jesus appears in the Gospel of Matthew as if clothed in the purple of heaven's royalty. For the kingdom he was born of the virgin Mary. For the kingdom he lived a sinless earthly life. For the kingdom he prayed, preached, wrought miracles, and taught his disciples. For the kingdom he suffered the darkness of Gethsemane, endured the unspeakable agony of Calvary's cross, and went to the depths of death and the grave.

For the kingdom he rose on the third day. For the kingdom he manifested himself through forty days, after which he ascended from Olivet's heights into heaven. For the kingdom he now is making intercession at the right hand of God. For the consummation of the kingdom he is coming back to earth again.

Jesus fulfilled all the promises of God for a messianic king. The word "Messiah" is a transliterated Hebrew word meaning anointed; the name "Christ" is a transliterated Greek word with the same meaning. Jesus was called the Anointed One, a term which his followers understood to refer to the messianic King. Peter boldly confessed: "Thou art the Christ, the Son of the living God" (Matt. 16:16).

Jesus refused to be enthroned as a king who had come to establish a political kingdom and throw off the yoke of Rome from Israel. He came to establish a spiritual kingdom, universal in its sweep, founded on love, which would be motivated by the rule of heaven in the hearts of men. His first recorded sermon theme was, "Repent: for the kingdom of heaven is at hand" (Matt. 4:17).

Often Jesus spoke of the kingdom as already in existence, as when he said: "Then the kingdom of God is come unto you" (Matt. 12:28). Often he pictured it as a progressive growth, "first the blade, then the ear, after that the full corn in the ear" (Mark 4:28). Jesus also spoke of the consummation of the kingdom as a future event: "For the Son of man shall come in the glory of his Father with his angels; and then he shall reward every man according to his works" (Matt. 16:27).

III. The Citizens of the Kingdom

People make up a kingdom. The kingdom of heaven comes from above; the citizens of the kingdom are on the earth. The authority of the King must be accepted by the human heart before one can enter the kingdom or be worthy to be called a citizen of the kingdom.

1. Entering the Kingdom

Our Lord said to Nicodemus: "Except a man be born of water and of the Spirit, he cannot enter into the kingdom of God. That which is born of the flesh is flesh; and that which is born of the Spirit is spirit. Marvel not that I said unto thee, Ye must be born again" (John 3:5-7). One cannot enter the kingdom without the new birth. This he experiences through the Holy Spirit when he puts his heartfelt trust in Jesus as sovereign Lord and Saviour.

After spending many months instructing his disciples in the principles of the kingdom of heaven, Jesus asked the twelve: "Whom say ye that I am?" (Matt. 16:15). That question is the crux of the whole matter. What relation to the King does one bear? What trust and love and loyalty does one have? Without renunciation of the rival king Satan, and without faith in the King, one cannot enter the kingdom.

2. Social Relationships in the Kingdom

Much of one's love, loyalty, and obedience to the King is shown by one's attitude toward others, that is, by social relationships.

This statement is not to deny that the new birth is a primary necessity. However, the new birth results in right conduct. Much of the Sermon on the Mount refers to a Christian's relationships to his fellow men. A social relationship is outlined in Matthew 18:15-17, the passage about reconciliation with one's brother through the aid of the church. It is significant that in the two recorded times that Jesus mentioned the church, the first (Matt. 16:18) speaks of its foundation and building and the second (Matt. 18:17) speaks of the social application of the gospel.

3. Greatness in the Kingdom

The disciples were greatly concerned about who would be the greatest in the kingdom; Jesus was greatly concerned that they should know what true greatness in the kingdom is. Breaking the commandments of the King and teaching others to do so is littleness in the kingdom; doing and teaching the King's commandments is greatness (Matt. 5:19). With exquisite tenderness Jesus rebuked the selfish ambition of the twelve, who wanted pre-eminence over others in the kingdom. He taught the revolutionary idea that greatness is attained through childlikeness (Matt. 18:1–6) and through service (Matt. 20:27–28). There are wide ranges of degrees of greatness in the kingdom of heaven.

4. Seeking the Kingdom

"Seek ye first the kingdom of God, and his righteousness" (Matt. 6:33), said Jesus. To seek to enter the kingdom should be man's earnest initial endeavor; to seek more and more to surrender to the reign of heaven in one's own life should be the Christian's continuing and fervent purpose; to seek to bring other men under the sovereignty of the King should be a kingdom man's incessant activity and joy.

The kingdom is described as a treasure in a field, so valuable that one should be willing to sell all that he has and joyously buy that field. It is described as the pearl of great price, which one should seek even though it cost him all of his treasures combined (Matt. 13:44–46).

A good kingdom citizen seeks to relate everything that he does directly or indirectly to the wish of the King and the program of the kingdom.

5. Receiving One's Inheritance

One who has come into the kingdom through the new birth is heir apparent to its full blessings. His capacity to receive and experience his inheritance is developed through various factors, one of which is his right conduct. In this sense the believer will be rewarded for good works by coming into his inheritance in the kingdom. Meanwhile, he rejoices in "an inheritance incorruptible, and undefiled, and that fadeth not away, reserved in heaven" for him. (1 Peter 1:4).

"Then shall the King say unto them on his right hand, Come, ye blessed of my Father, *inherit* [author's italics] the kingdom prepared for you from the foundation of the world: For I was an hungered, and ye gave me meat: I was thirsty, and ye gave me drink: I was a stranger, and ye took me in: naked, and ye clothed me: I was sick, and ye visited me: I was in prison, and ye came unto me."

This passage cannot mean entrance into the kingdom through good works. However, one who has come into the kingdom through the new birth may be rewarded for good works by having an enlarged capacity to appropriate his inheritance in the kingdom. The heartfelt hope of all devoted followers of Christ is that they may hear from him the welcome plaudit: "Well done, thou good and faithful servant: thou hast been faithful over a few things, I will make thee ruler over many things: enter thou into the joy of thy lord" (Matt. 25:21).

IV. THE PROCLAMATION OF THE KINGDOM

Christians love their churches because Jesus is alive and active in the midst of them. He has committed to the churches the supernal task of advancing the kingdom of heaven under the directing power of the Holy Spirit.

The church is not synonymous with the kingdom, although

the two are closely related. "Kingdom" is a translation of the Greek word *basileia*, meaning "rule" or "reign." "Church" is a translation of the Greek word *ecclesia*, meaning "an assembly" or "those who are called out." The word for church occurs only in Matthew among the four Gospel writers and is used by him only three times (Matt. 16:18; 18:17).

When Jesus first mentioned the church (Matt. 16:18–19) he committed to it "the keys of the kingdom of heaven." The keys are to open the doors of the kingdom for men to enter. Thus Jesus committed to the churches the divine task of soul-winning and evangelism and world missions.

The New Testament church is the divinely appointed agent for the proclamation of the kingdom. The continuing command of the risen King to his churches is to go, to make disciples of all nations, to baptize, and to teach (Matt. 28:18–20). The church that is doing so is a living, faithful, victorious agent of the King. Only those who are willing to dedicate themselves to Christ and his kingdom-building program have any scriptural justification for belonging to a New Testament church.

V. THE GROWTH OF THE KINGDOM

Approximately one third of the people on earth are nominally Christian or of Christian inclination. This is a far cry from the little group on a Galilean hillside who heard the King's commission to make disciples of all nations. By what power has the kingdom grown?

By the fourth century, Christians had become so numerous and influential that Constantine, the Roman emperor, thought it politically expedient to make Christianity the official religion of the Roman Empire. Why did Christianity sweep like a tidal wave over Europe, light the cities and forests of Britain, inhabit the plains and mountains of America with followers of the King, and move restlessly in all directions toward the uttermost parts of the earth?

Christianity has spread because the kingdom of heaven is a spiritual movement, empowered by the Holy Spirit and promoted by the churches to exalt the living Christ as King and Saviour of men. It is neither a political movement nor a conquest by force. It is not primarily economic, educational, social, nor philosophical. It is a conquest of love, an influence of character, a movement of the Spirit of God within the hearts of men. If people take Christ to rule over their lives, others soon begin to feel the divine presence. Nothing is more contagious. The kingdom of heaven is like leaven that leavens the whole lump of society (Matt. 13:33).

VI. THE PRIMACY OF THE KINGDOM

Christ the King in perfect love challenges devoted fidelity to himself as sovereign Lord. He commands, "Seek ye first the kingdom." To surrender to the lordship of Jesus is not like surrendering in defeat before some aggressive enemy. It is as when a sick patient surrenders to a good physician who can do more than the sick man can do for himself.

One repents, changes his mind and his allegiance, when he sees that the King's way is better than his own way. The abundant life is experienced when the Lord Christ has absolute control over one's will, control of one's economic life, control of one's relationships with his fellow men, and control of one's loyalties. It is life under an absolute monarchy of divine grace and goodness.

Life in the kingdom of heaven is a surrender of earth's offerings in order to enjoy the riches as a child of the King. One attains this abundant life when Christ is Lord of all; it cannot be experienced if the sovereign is given second place.

VII. THE PROMISED CONSUMMATION OF THE KINGDOM

Paul described the conquering King of the kingdom of heaven when he ascended into heaven, leading sin and death as captives, and having gifts in his hand for his faithful. "When he ascended up on high, he led captivity captive, and gave gifts unto men" (Eph. 4:8).

Even greater glory is yet promised. The King has promised to come to the earth a second time, in power and great glory, with rewards for his faithful subjects (Matt. 16:27). Heavenly voices will shout with a paean of praise that "the kingdom of the world is become the kingdom of our Lord, and of his Christ: and he shall reign for ever and ever" (Rev. 11:15, ASV).

Jesus came first in weakness; he will come again in power. He came in humility; he will return in great glory. He came as a babe in Bethlehem; he will come again as the King of the kingdom. He came to be Saviour; he will return to judge and rule. He was reviled and rejected by men; to him every kingdom of the world is become the kingdom of our Lord, He came to wear a crown of thorns and be crucified; he will return to wear the royal diadem and be glorified.

FOR RESEARCH AND DISCUSSION

1. Let each member of the class give his own definition of the kingdom of heaven.
2. What effect did the Babylonian captivity, the conquest by Syria between the times of the Old and New Testaments, and the conquest by Rome, have on Jewish hopes for a messianic king?
3. What were some errors in the minds of the disciples when they quarreled over who would be greatest in the kingdom?
4. Will heaven hereafter be exactly the same for all who are in the kingdom? Discuss degrees of rewards.
5. Is the kingdom of heaven growing as rapidly as the population of the world?
6. Why did Jesus not foretell the exact time when he is coming back to the earth?

CHAPTER 3

I. ANCESTRY OF JESUS THE KING (1:1–17)
  1. Royal Lineage Given by Matthew
  2. Born of Sinners
  3. Born a King in Answer to Prophecy
  4. Born in the Fulness of Time
  5. Born at the End of the Line

II. BIRTH OF THE KING (1:18–25)
  1. Miracle of the Holy Spirit (1:18)
  2. Nobility of Joseph (1:19)
  3. Revelation in a Dream (1:20–21)
  4. Fulfilment of Prophecy (1:22–23)
  5. Birth of the Royal Babe (1:24–25)

III. ADORATION AND ANTAGONISM (2:1–23)
  1. Magi Adoring the Little King (2:1–2, 9–12)
  2. Herod Hating the Little King (2:3–8, 13–23)

IV. PREPARATION AND INAUGURATION (3:1–17)
  1. John the Baptist Preaching the Kingdom (3:1–12)
  2. Baptizing the King (3:13–15)
  3. Deity Anointing and Acknowledging the King (3:16–17)

V. CLASH WITH THE RIVAL KING (4:1–11)
  1. Tempted to Use Materialistic Power (4:1–4)
  2. Tempted to Employ Spectacular Display (4:5–7)
  3. Tempted by a View of the Present World Order (4:8–11)

VI. LAUNCHING THE KINGDOM MOVEMENT (4:12–25)
  1. Proclaiming the Kingdom as at Hand (4:12–17)
  2. Enlisting Kingdom Men (4:18–25)

3

The King Comes to Establish
the Kingdom

Matthew 1–4

MORE than one hundred names, titles, or designations are ascribed to Jesus Christ in the Bible. None is more appropriate than King. As King he has had a retinue of angels, saints, and martyrs—noble characters more splendid than any who ever attended an earthly sovereign's court. He has had enemies to his authority more dangerous than any who ever beseiged a walled city or sought to win a throne by intrigue. He maintains a rule of love more dynamic than dictatorship and more compelling than force.

I. ANCESTRY OF JESUS THE KING (1:1–17)

The genealogy of Jesus is intriguing and inspiring. Matthew begins with Abraham, since he was writing principally to Jews. He divides the list into three fourteens, presumably for the sake of easy memory. However, he lists only forty-one names, for he makes an event in history one dividing point.

David is the first point of division, for here the royal line of Jesus began. The carrying away into captivity is the next point of division, for there the seed of David ceased to rule on the throne. Matthew beautifully combines the natural with the miraculous as he gives the human ancestry of Jesus along with a forceful account of his divine origin.

1. *Royal Lineage Given by Matthew*

Matthew's genealogy of Jesus is different from Luke's.

There are many theories accounting for the difference. The most reasonable and satisfying explanation is that Matthew gives the lineage of Joseph, which would be the legal Jewish genealogy of Jesus, whereas Luke gives the ancestry of Mary —from whom Luke probably received his information.

Jesus is portrayed in Matthew's list as being specifically in the line of kings. He was born exactly as the Saviour of the world should be born. He was born of a woman, that he might be identified with humanity; he was born of the Holy Spirit, that he might be God come down to bring men his grace and glory.

2. Born of Sinners

The charts of Jesus' ancestry include names of men and women who gave way to sin: Abraham, Jacob, David, Solomon, Manasseh, and Jeconiah—to mention a few whose sins flash before memory at the mention of the name. His family tree has names of women such as Tamar the adulteress, Ruth the pagan Gentile, Rahab the harlot, Bathsheba, whom David took from her husband Uriah. With such a heritage, the sinlessness of Jesus' life is all the more marvelous in our eyes.

3. Born a King in Answer to Prophecy

The prophetic gleam foretelling the Messiah grew bright in the life and work of Moses; it was dramatized in the priestly functions of the tabernacle and Temple; it was blazoned against the dark skies of ancient Israel by the prophets from Isaiah to Malachi. The messianic hope was fanned into flame with the Babylonian captivity, with the Maccabean period of conflict with Syria during interbiblical history, and during the occupation of Palestine by Rome after 63 B.C.

Israel's "hopes and fears of all the years" met in Jesus Christ, the King of the kingdom of heaven. Matthew traces

THE KING COMES TO ESTABLISH THE KINGDOM 19

the Lord's ancestry to show Jesus to be the fulfilment of God's continuing promise given first to Abraham and to show him to be the heir to the eternal throne which God had promised David.

4. Born in the Fulness of Time

Many ideologies had been tried and had failed. The Hebrew people had experienced the patriarchal plan under Abraham and his successors, theocratic government under the judges, and monarchy under David and his descendants. These all failed to bring abundant life to the people.

Egypt with her science, Babylon with her mysticism, Greece with her democracy and cultural arts, Rome with her universal law—all these failed to satisfy the spiritual yearnings in the hearts of men. Pericles built no enduring kingdom, even with his philosophy and fine arts. Alexander built no enduring kingdom, even with his world-conquering military exploits. The Caesars built no enduring kingdom, even with their law courts and cessation of war.

Plato spoke for the waiting world when he said: "We wait for one, be it God or God-inspired man, to teach us our duty and to wipe the darkness from our eyes." Jesus came in "the fulness of the time" (Gal. 4:4).

5. Born at the End of the Line

Jesus is "the Alpha and Omega." He is the first of the new creation, the God-man; he is the completion of the old order. He is both the Ancient of Days and the Rock of Ages, both the Lion of the Tribe of Judah and the Lamb of God.

II. BIRTH OF THE KING (1:18–25)

One of the most eloquent and moving sounds on earth is the cry of a newborn babe. When a man child is born to royalty, the cry may take on global significance. The birth of the King of the kingdom of heaven was eternally significant.

1. *Miracle of the Holy Spirit* (1:18)

Matthew intimates (v. 16) that Jesus was not the son of Joseph. With inspired delicacy he then proceeds to tell of the miracle. Mary is introduced as being engaged to Joseph but not having taken him as her husband.

Comparatively little is known about Mary, her parents, her childhood, or her education; more is known about her character. She was a young woman of rare spirituality, humbly rejoicing in the high favor she had found with God to become the mother of the Messiah. She was thoroughly versed in the Old Testament Scriptures. Indeed she was "blessed among women."

There is no scriptural justification for worshiping her or praying to her or seeking her intercession with Christ, but there is every reason to admire her character and piety and purity. Yet her glory is a reflected glory, the glory of her miraculously born Son.

"Before they came together she was found to be with child of the Holy Spirit" (1:18, RSV). We do not know all that is meant. Clearly, this birth was unlike any other birth in history.

An unbelieving physician once sought to ensnare the author before a crowd by asking him: "Parson, recently a young woman in our hospital gave birth to a boy, declaring that the child had no human father. Would you have believed her story?"

The question caught my breath for a moment! But breathing a prayer, I answered about as follows: "Doctor, if that mother's son had been born in exact fulfilment of prophecy for some fifteen hundred years; if the stars of the heavens and the angels above had acknowledged the glory of it; if Wise Men had come from afar to worship him and bring gifts; if his life had been so sinless that even his bitterest enemies could not convict him of one sin; if his hands had healed the lepers and opened blind eyes; if he had called forth the dead from the grave; if he had spoken such words of wisdom that the world would sit at his feet listening; if cruel men had crucified him on a cross and the very sun had hidden its face for shame at the deed; if a platoon of soldiers guarding his grave could not prevent his rising from the dead; if for forty days he had manifested his resurrection by many infallible proofs; if he had done for me what One has done who was born without a human father—if all this had been true, oh, yes, Doctor, I would believe that mother's story."

2. *Nobility of Joseph* (1:19)

Joseph was an upright man. In order to avoid disgracing Mary, he decided to break the engagement and put her away as quietly as possible. In Jewish custom, being betrothed was a legal tie. Unfaithfulness was considered adultery worthy of stoning (Deut. 22:23f). Joseph considered divorcing Mary quietly without public demonstration, but as a wise and good man he decided to sleep over his problem. God took a hand in the difficult and delicate affair.

3. *Revelation in a Dream* (1:20-21)

Joseph went to sleep with a troubled mind and heavy heart, doubtless praying. It was a glorious time for an angel of God to appear. The angelic messenger in the dream addressed Joseph as a son of David the king, and told him about David's greater Son who was to be born. The angel bade Joseph not to fear to marry Mary, for that which was conceived in her was of the Holy Spirit. It was delicately fitting that God should have revealed the miraculous secret to Mary first—as told by Luke—and then to Joseph when her condition became apparent.

A baby's name is always important. The angel proclaimed

the eternal significance in naming the King of the kingdom of heaven. He was to be named Jesus. This was a familiar Jewish name, "Jesus" being the Greek form of the Hebrew name "Joshua" or "Jeshua" or "Jeshu." It means "Jehovah is helper," or "Help of Jehovah" or "Jehovah is salvation." Jesus was to save the people from their sins, that is, from the guilt and penalty of sin, from the power of temptation to sin, from sin and from sinning. This salvation was infinitely more heavenly than the Jewish hope for deliverance from the domination of a foreign country.

4. Fulfilment of Prophecy (1:22-23)

The event of the birth of Christ was both timely and timeless in significance. It came to pass in fulfilment of the prophecy of Isaiah (7:14): "Behold, a virgin shall conceive, and bear a son, and shall call his name Immanuel." The name, Immanuel, meaning "God with us," is one of the most beautiful and meaningful of the names ascribed unto Jesus.

> I know not how that Bethlehem's Babe
> Could in the God-head be;
> I only know the Manger Child
> Has brought God's life to me.
>
> I know not how that Calvary's cross
> A world from sin could free:
> I only know its matchless love
> Has brought God's love to me.
>
> H. W. FARRINGTON

5. Birth of the Royal Babe (1:24-25)

Noble and obedient, Joseph did as the angelic messenger had said. He took the gentle Mary to be his wife and "knew her not till she had brought forth a son" (ASV). Their secret revelation from God seems not to have been made public. It was perfectly natural that the people of Nazareth thought of Jesus as the son of Joseph, and natural for Mary to say, "Thy father and I" (Luke 2:48).

The chronology marking A.D. and B.C.—worked out by Dionysius Exiguus in the sixth century—is known to be in error. Apparently, Herod died in 4 B.C. A decree ordering a census went out from Rome late in 8 B.C. It probably took much time to be executed in the remote sections of the Roman Empire. Jesus probably was born in 5 B.C. or a year earlier.

III. ADORATION AND ANTAGONISM (2:1–23)

The star of Bethlehem shed its brightness over the little town which was nestled on the east side of one of Judea's hills. Motherhood and childhood and Saviourhood were forever sanctified in that scene. So startling were the manifestations of the supernatural that kings and wise men of the earth were agitated into action.

1. Magi Adoring the Little King (2:1–2, 9–12)

A tradition, accepted by some early Christians, says that the Magi were kings. That tradition probably grew out of such messianic prophecy as Psalm 68:29: "Because of thy temple at Jerusalem shall kings bring presents unto thee." Neither Matthew nor Luke calls them kings. They were Wise Men, or Magi. These were the scholars, the teachers, the scientists, the astrologers of the priestly class of the people of the East. It was natural that they should go first to Herod, the king in the capital of the country, when they were seeking a newborn king.

Throughout the East there was widespread expectation even among the Gentiles that a mighty Jewish king would appear. These expectations doubtless arose from the Jewish prophets and spread everywhere among the learned.

The Magi knew of the expectation and could study the

stars for a sign. It has been conjectured that the star which they saw was a conjunction of Jupiter and Saturn. More likely it was supernatural, for Matthew 2:9 says that the star "went before them, till it came and stood over where the young child was."

All the earth was waiting, spent and restless, watching for the coming of the King. The Magi realized that "the desire of all nations" had appeared. Herod was greatly troubled at their report; Jerusalem was excited. Herod learned from the chief priests and scribes where the Messiah was expected to be born. (See Micah 5:2.) Matthew gives a free translation, using the word "governor," indicating one who governs and also protects his people.

No wonder the Magi rejoiced! Egypt was yearning for more than her learning could give. India desired something more than her wealth could buy. Greece hungered for an inner spiritual culture which her philosophers and artists had never attained. Israel's need was for a king of righteousness and peace and for spiritual deliverance. The Magi found the hope for all these in the newborn King. They worshiped with a homage which was given only to a king. They brought gold, a fitting gift for a king. They brought frankincense, the incense usually offered to their deities. They brought myrrh, which signified death because it was used in embalming.

Being warned of God, the Wise Men made their way eastward across the fords of the Jordan, without returning to Jerusalem, where the treachery of Herod would have entrapped them. The Magi went back with a gift far greater than they brought; they had found the gift of God, the King of the kingdom of heaven.

2. *Herod Hating the Little King* (2:3–8, 13–23)

Christ is ever the dividing Christ, separating those who adore him from those who hate him. The contrast is seen in the comparison of the Magi with Herod.

Herod (called Herod the Great) was part Idumaean, part Jew. He was appointed king of Judea by the Roman Senate in 40 B.C., having been sponsored by Anthony. He gained full sovereignty in 37 B.C. Herod's infamous reign is a dark page of history. Through jealousy for his throne he slew many of the relatives of his wife, Mariamne, who was a descendant of the Maccabees. Eventually he ordered the death of Mariamne herself—seemingly the only person he ever loved—and later of his mother-in-law. Finally he had his own two sons, Alexander and Aristobulus, killed because he was jealous of the throne.

The Emperor Augustus is quoted as having said: "It is safer to be Herod's pig (Greek, *hus*) than to be his son (Greek, *huios*)."

Knowing Herod's record, one can understand his excited, savage jealousy when Wise Men from afar came asking for one "that is born King of the Jews." Herod's murderous nature was aroused to fury. His political fears were unfounded; well should he have felt godly fear of the spiritual power of the newborn King.

Just as Herod was thwarted by God's revelation to the Magi, so was he thwarted again in his mad purpose by a dream sent to Joseph. The psalmist had said: "The kings of the earth set themselves, and the rulers take counsel together, against the Lord, and against his anointed. . . . He that sitteth in the heavens shall laugh: the Lord shall have them in derision" (Psalm 2:2–4).

Obeying God's warning, Joseph made a hasty and secret departure by night into Egypt. It was a journey of about one hundred miles to the heart of Egypt—about as far as Jesus ever traveled from the place of his birth. Egypt was a province of the Roman Empire, well governed, and outside the jurisdiction of Herod. There were many Jews there, enjoying full liberty.

Matthew, anxious to show his Jewish readers that Jesus

fulfilled the Old Testament prophecies, quoted Hosea 11:1: "I . . . called my son out of Egypt," (cf. Matt. 2:15). Hosea was speaking primarily of the nation Israel, but under the Spirit's inspiration he also foretold this experience in the life of Jesus. Joseph and Mary remained in Egypt, guarding the babe until the jealous old Herod died.

It was not likely that Herod, a master in the art of wholesale "purges," would let a threat to his throne go by without trying to kill the potential rival. Taking no chances, he had the male babies in Bethlehem slain. It is not recounted just how many babies were killed, but the sound of the weeping of mothers must have reached every ear. True to his style, Matthew quotes the Old Testament prophet when he referred to the time when Nebuchadnezzar carried the people into captivity: "Rahel weeping for her children" (Jer. 31: 15). The prophet used poetic language about the nation; Matthew used it concerning Bethlehem. Jewish people knew that the tomb of Rachel was near Bethlehem.

The wretched old Herod died. Joseph dreamed again. God told him to return to the land of Israel, since the one who had sought to kill the child was dead. Even then the southern part of the land of Israel was not safe. Herod's son, Archelaus, was ruling Judea and living in Jerusalem. Like father, like son. (Old Herod had ten wives and many children, most of them showing a bad strain of blood.)

In another dream God warned Joseph to take the mother and child to Galilee, outside the reach of Archelaus, since Herod Antipas of Galilee was not so notoriously cruel. In Nazareth of Galilee Jesus was to spend about thirty years, preparing for his ministry. Like Bethlehem, the little town has been ever glorified through association with his name.

IV. PREPARATION AND INAUGURATION (3:1-17)

Events in the childhood and young manhood of the most amazing personality in history would be intriguing to know.

One wonders about the home life, school disciplines, social adjustments, and religious training of Jesus. Many fanciful— sometimes absurd or actually blasphemous—legends about the childhood of Jesus have grown up. None is worth repeating.

Only Luke gives the story about Jesus in the Temple when he was twelve years old, and adds that he "increased in wisdom and stature, and in favour with God and man" (Luke 2:52). Mark says that people called him a carpenter, a name which he may have received by growing up in the home of Joseph.

The usual assumption is that Jesus followed Joseph's trade. However, some Bible students think that Jesus may have worked on a farm, perhaps apprenticed to a tiller of the soil. He used no illustration about carpentering except rare references about building a house or barn or tower. He constantly talked about sowing, plowing, reaping harvests, treasures in fields, dogs, birds, foxes, vineyards, clouds, kinds of soil, seed, and dozens of things with which a farmer boy would be most familiar.

Matthew skips over nearly thirty years of Jesus' life story. Why? It was not pertinent to his theme.

1. *John the Baptist Preaching the Kingdom* (3:1–12)

Dynamic, Spirit-filled, authoritative preaching has always drawn listeners. John the Baptist was doing some dynamic and pertinent preaching by the Jordan, just north of the Dead Sea. For some four hundred long and spiritually dry years since the time of Malachi no such voice of a prophet had been heard.

John's ministry was the fulfilment of Isaiah's prophecy of one who should cut down the hills, fill up the valleys, straighten out the curves, to make a spiritual road for the coming of the King (Isa. 40:3–5).

John's preaching was startling. Judgment! Fire! The axe

ready to dig up and cut down fruitless trees! Thresh out the wheat; gather the good; burn the chaff! Flee the wrath to come! The kingdom of heaven is at hand—as close as one's right hand—and the King is about to appear! Repent, change your minds and your ways; show by your way of living that you have repented! The coming King will baptize in the fire of judgment; he will save the righteous like good wheat; he will burn the chaff in unquenchable (Greek, *asbestos*) fire! Repent, and be baptized!

We never heard such preaching before, said many of the Jews within themselves. They were baptized in throngs. When a committee of Pharisees and Sadducees came out from Jerusalem, either to investigate John or through curiosity, he did not address them as "beloved brethren." He called them a brood of snakes. The hypocritical morality of some of the leading Pharisees and the smug skepticism of many of the Sadducees gave John the opportunity to preach repentance and the judgment.

John the Baptist pointed men to Jesus, urging them to obey the King of righteousness and to enter the kingdom of heaven. The Jews constantly boasted that one descended from Abraham need not fear the judgment of God. John said God could raise up children to Abraham by turning stones into men, if necessary. People thronged to accept the baptism of repentance. John immersed his converts in the Jordan River.

2. Baptizing the King (3:13–15)

Jesus came to John and asked for baptism. John was conscious of being in the presence of deity, and he modestly demurred. He felt that it would be more appropriate for Jesus to baptize him. But Jesus' course was necessary in order "to fulfil all righteousness." Jesus' example of fulfilling all righteousness is worthy of all acceptance.

Matthew states that Jesus "went up straightway out of the

water." The word *baptizo* in all Greek dictionaries and literature means immersion. One can see in baptism the prophetic symbolism of Christ's burial and resurrection. His baptism was a sort of inauguration ceremony for Jesus and the climax of John's ministry. John was to Jesus like the morning star presaging the rising of the sun in its splendor.

3. Deity Anointing and Acknowledging the King (3:16-17)

The King was about to begin his public ministry. Three divine manifestations came: (1) The heavens opened, showing the King's realm of sovereignty. (2) The Holy Spirit descended upon him in the form of a dove, indicating the spiritual nature of his rule. (3) God the Father spoke, revealing the favor of the Almighty upon his kingdom program.

The opening of the heavens was clearly a miraculous providence, appropriate for this high occasion. The form of a dove was seen by Jesus and John, but it is not certain that others saw it. The coming of the Holy Spirit upon Jesus was like his anointing into his kingship. The language of the heavenly voice, "This is my beloved Son, in whom I am well pleased," indicated that God had delighted in him from the beginning of eternity. Each person of the Trinity—Father, Son, and Holy Spirit—was manifested in this holy scene.

V. CLASH WITH THE RIVAL KING (4:1-11)

Many kings, such as Julius Caesar and Augustus, were forced to conquer their rivals in order to attain their kingdoms. The King who came to win the hearts of men met his rival claimant in terrific combat. Jesus was led by the Spirit into the wilderness to be tempted by the devil. During the trial, Jesus fasted forty days.

No one can truthfully say that he was ever more sorely tempted than was Jesus. Satan appeared as a real personality. The Bible represents Satan as the chief of the fallen angels, always hating God, always working on God's territory, trying to lead God's children into disobedience and rebellion. Each temptation of Jesus was related directly to the kingship of the kingdom of heaven.

1. Tempted to Use Materialistic Power (4:1–4)

"Command that these stones be made bread," suggested Satan. "If thou be the Son of God" was a direct thrust at God's providential care, suggesting that God should not allow his Son to hunger. This temptation was an unworthy appeal to Jesus to use his miraculous power for a selfish purpose. Though hunger was natural, Jesus would not use his sovereign power for himself. He refused to turn stones into loaves. This temptation came again when Jesus fed the five thousand by a miracle and the people wanted to make him their military deliverer. Behold, thought they, he could feed the army without a commissary department!

The Scriptures were "the sword of the Spirit" by which Jesus conquered his rival: "Man shall not live by bread alone" (cf. Deut. 8:3). Men with the rule of heaven in their hearts must not put material things foremost. Men must not seek to become kingdom citizens for materialistic gain. Jesus refused to establish his kingdom primarily on an economic or materialistic basis.

2. Tempted to Employ Spectacular Display (4:5–7)

The first temptation was to the body; the second one was to ambition. The first was to use God's power for self; the second was to use his power presumptuously. Spurious pretenders for the messiahship sought to manifest themselves as wonder-workers. That was the expectation of the people.

The pinnacle of the Temple was a spectacular place from which to throw oneself among the milling crowd. Satan suggested to Jesus that this would be a most dramatic and sensational way to announce his kingship. The devil even quoted from the Scriptures (Psalm 91:11f), though he misinterpreted the words. Jesus refused to presume on God's protecting power. He would not become king by spectacular display. Drawing the sword of the Spirit, Jesus quoted: "Thou shalt not tempt the Lord thy God" (cf. Deut. 6:16).

3. Tempted by a View of the Present World Order (4:8–11)

The battle of the ages was fought on a high mountain from which Jesus was shown the kingdoms of the world with their glory. A rugged, barren, miserably hot mountain northwest of Jericho, called Quarantania, is the traditional mount of temptation.

Both of the rival kings wanted universal sovereignty. Satan claimed that the kingdoms of the world were his. For once he told the truth. He is called "the Prince of this world" (John 12:31). This world order of ignorance, poverty, sin, and death is his domain.

Satan was in danger of losing his kingdom to the King of righteousness, unless he could bring Jesus to his own terms. He offered the kingdom on condition that Jesus worship him. As in the other temptations, Jesus drove the devil off with the Word of God (see Deut. 6:13). With the rival king at his back, Jesus looked toward the time when the kingdom of this world order would become the kingdom of our Lord and his Christ (Rev. 11:15). Angels came and ministered unto him.

VI. LAUNCHING THE KINGDOM MOVEMENT (4:12–25)

On the pinnacle of victory over his rival, Jesus was ready to launch his campaign for winning his kingdom. Matthew relates only that portion of the life of Christ that pertains to his subject: the King and the kingdom of heaven. He waits until later in the narrative to tell why John was delivered up to imprisonment and death. He first relates that Jesus moved into Galilee and selected Capernaum rather than Nazareth as an advantageous place for his headquarters.

1. *Proclaiming the Kingdom as at Hand* (4:12–17)

The resounding trumpets of heaven must have pealed forth triumphantly when Jesus went forth preaching, "Repent: for the kingdom of heaven is at hand." John the Baptist had heralded the same kingdom message. John was austere, ascetic, severe; Jesus was gentle, winsome, magnetic. This, the first text used by the Messiah, was his unwavering text through life, his abiding text until the end.

His kingdom was not geographical, not militaristic, not political; it was spiritual. The burden of his message was: "Change your minds and change your ways, change your master, let heaven rule in your hearts. The kingdom of heaven is at hand; the King is here." It was welcome news indeed, glad tidings, the gospel.

2. *Enlisting Kingdom Men* (4:18–25)

Significantly, Jesus chose ordinary men as his kingdom subjects—fishermen and the like—rather than rabbis, Pharisees, scribes, and Sadducees. He needed men who were not bound by the traditions of the ages and the prejudices of the people, men who were thoughtful but teachable. He knew the frailties of these men, but he knew their possibilities as leaders of the people.

With regal authority Jesus called them to follow him, saying, "Follow me, and I will make you fishers of men." The parallelism between fishing and soul-winning is striking. Both require skill, patience, persistance, courage, love, knowledge of the habits of those to be "caught," and the ability to fit the appeal to the catch.

Jesus made a circle tour of the Galilean cities and villages, teaching, healing, preaching. He preached "the gospel of the kingdom." Galilee was thickly populated, with numerous cities and villages. News about such preaching and such healing of diseases spread like fire in the breeze, reaching out from Galilee into Jerusalem and all Judea to the south, into Decapolis east of the Jordan, even as far as Syria. The expectant world was anxious to hear this prophet who was preaching that the kingdom of heaven was at hand. What a king he would make, feeding armies and poor people by miracles, healing the wounded and sick by speaking the word, driving out demons and blessing people of high and low estate! People came from all directions.

FOR RESEARCH AND DISCUSSION

1. What bearing does the virgin birth have on the deity of Christ?
2. Try to list the principal prophecies fulfilled in the events surrounding the birth of Jesus.
3. Does God speak to people through dreams now? What dangers are involved in looking for communication through dreams?
4. How was Herod's realm divided among his sons? Why did Joseph feel safer under Antipas than under Archelaus?
5. Why was Jesus baptized, since he had no sins to be forgiven? What is the difference between his baptism and ours?
6. How was Jesus tempted in *all* points like as we are?

CHAPTER 4

4

The Way of Life in the Kingdom

WHEN a national political party in America meets every four years, the first thing the delegates do is to outline a platform of principles telling how the party leaders propose to regulate the way of life in the nation. Next, they nominate a candidate for president. They say to the people, "Elect our man and we will govern the nation according to our platform." In a similar way the Sermon on the Mount gives a summary of the way of living proposed by Jesus the King.

This sermon is not a sum total of all the beliefs and practices of the Christian faith. It has been called the Magna Carta of the kingdom, the manifesto of Jesus, the ordination sermon of the twelve, and other names. It describes in simple language the principles which ought to prevail in the lives of men after they come into the kingdom of heaven. Whether Jesus uttered all these truths consecutively, or whether Matthew has given a compilation of many messages of Jesus is a question for scholars.

The sermon does not tell how to enter the kingdom; the disciples were already in. It does not give a complete system of morals—everything one should know and practice in the kingdom. It is an error to say that the Sermon on the Mount is all the religion that anyone needs. Yet in its exalted truth, beautiful simplicity, profound depth, and wide range one learns the inner spirit and general principles of the kingdom. Christendom would be shocked if one should openly denounce its teachings; perhaps it would be more shocked if one should obey its principles completely.

I. THE KINGDOM WAY OF HAPPINESS (5:1–12)

Jesus began his discourse by answering one of the universal questions of mankind—how to be happy. Through the ages men have wanted inner peace and joy. They have gone into many blind alleys of failure in their search. Most of the sins and many of the sorrows of life have come from the wrong way of pursuing happiness. Christ has the secret. Yet so few people take his plan seriously. The first falsehood Satan usually tells young people who are contemplating accepting Jesus is that to do so will rob them of happiness.

Worldly people seek happiness from without—by getting things, going places, accumulating wealth, gaining fame, enjoying popularity, having thrills. Happiness must always work from the heart; it cannot depend on outward circumstances. It is tragic that Christians sometimes let circumstances control, that they lose the radiance of the Christian experience, that they let the glow go, that they fail to enjoy the spirit of the Beatitudes. These Beatitudes give the secret of inner, spiritual happiness that is superior to circumstances.

If one has the kingdom of heaven in his heart, if he is comforted, if he inherits the earth, if his hunger and thirst after righteousness are satisfied, if he obtains mercy, if he sees God, if he is called the son of God, if he has the reign of Christ in his heart—if all these things are true of him, will he not be happy? The blessedness of the Beatitudes includes all that is implied in the words "happiness," "joy," "felicity," "inward peace." The eight Beatitudes are the octave of kingdom music. They are like an eight-rung ladder upon which one can climb to the delectable heights of Christian radiance and peace and joyous living.

One can easily imagine the surprise, unbelief, shock, and even disgust of some of those hearers when Jesus spoke of poverty, mourning, hunger, and meekness as elements which would bring happiness. People thought those things brought misery. With striking paradoxes and startling phrases Jesus taught the truth.

"Oh, the blessedness of the poor in spirit!" The poor in spirit are those who feel their abject poverty of spiritual resources, so that their utter dependence is upon God. The reign of the heavenly King begins in the heart when one acknowledges his own helplessness and his complete dependence upon the power from above.

"Oh, the blessedness of those who mourn!" must have shocked those hearers afresh, unless they realized that Jesus was talking about mourning and sorrow for sin. Jesus wept over the people of Jerusalem, then went out to die to save those very people. Those who help men out of sin into righteous living are the happiest of people.

"Oh, the blessedness of the meek!" may be even more startling to some today than then. Meekness is not weakness. Jesus meant self-control, not spinelessness; he meant positive humility, not negative timidity; he meant a spirit under the control of God, not a shrinking soul. Meekness connotes being disciplined to follow the direction of God. Meek people have been called the "terrible meek" because they always conquer. They inherit the earth. Moses and Jesus were the meekest of men, but they were the mightiest of men.

"Oh, the blessedness of hungering and thirsting after righteousness!" Every man in the depths of his soul should want to be righteous toward men as well as toward God. To seek righteousness is a divinely inspired quest.

Righteousness cannot be hidden. Jesus mentioned three results of righteousness which will be seen of others and which will add happiness to the heart: pity, purity, and peacemaking.

"Happy are the merciful," those who have pity. Jesus taught his disciples to pray, "Forgive us our debts, as we forgive our debtors," (Matt. 6:12), indicating that Christians may expect to experience God's forgiveness according to the way they have forgiven men. An unforgiving heart is always a heavy heart.

"Happy are the pure in heart" because their vision is capable of seeing God. One's physical vision depends upon the condition of his eye; one's spiritual vision depends upon the condition of his heart. God is purity; only the pure in heart are capable of seeing God in his majestic beauty.

"Blessed are the peacemakers," not, "Blessed are the warmakers." One who is devoted to peacemaking is so Godlike that he is called the son of God. Soul-winning is the happiest privilege given to Christians, because that is making peace between men and their forgiving God.

Happy are the "persecuted for righteousness' sake." Jesus amazed his disciples by speaking of the blessedness of righteous endurance under ill-treatment. Not all the persecuted are happy, only those who are persecuted for righteousness' sake. Christian character often incites ridicule, hostility, mockery, ostracism, ill-use, and insult from the ungodly. Hebrews 11:35–38 reveals this truth in vivid words.

Jesus said rejoice, "leap exceedingly" in joy, for such persecution associates one with the notable prophets. It associates one with the Saviour, for he "was despised and rejected of men." It associates one with Paul, for he suffered perils "above measure" (2 Cor. 11:23–28). In persecution Christians often find their supreme opportunity to witness for Christ. Possibly the King needs a faithful martyr or two today to advance his kingdom.

Christian experience bears witness to the truth of Christ's beatitudes. The only royal road to happiness is by character within.

> If happiness hae not her seat
> An' centre in the breast,

We may be wise, or rich, or great,
But never can be blest!

ROBERT BURNS

II. THE KINGDOM WAY OF INFLUENCE (5:13–16)

Desire for happiness and desire for influence are innate in the human heart. The happy Christian is an influential Christian, and vice versa. Few things are as contageous as radiant Christian living. There is a clarion call for the influence of sincere Christianity.

1. *Like Salt* (5:13)

The striking metaphor of Jesus is clear as one thinks of the purifying, preserving, and seasoning power of salt. It is terrifying to think of a society without some Christian influence. Without it the whole world would go into moral decay, into unrighteous putrefaction.

What is the savor of the salt, of which Jesus spoke? What is it that a Christian may have at one time and later lose? Certainly it is not the salvation of his soul. (Cf. John 10:28.) The savor of the salt is what we call spirituality.

It is the spiritually minded Christian who is influential. Without sincere spirituality, those who profess to be followers of Jesus Christ will be trodden under the feet of ridicule, scorn, and contempt. A spiritual Christian radiates holiness and happiness. Only a close walk with Jesus can keep the saltiness of Christian living effective, and thereby preserve society. Christ in us, like the savor of the salt, can make life "taste so good."

2. *Like Light* (5:14–16)

Probably Jesus pointed to a village high on a hill when he said, "Ye are the light of the world." People always see a light, especially in the dark. So will the dark world be lighted by Christian spirituality.

What is the candlestick for one's Christian light? In Revelation 1:12–13 the candlesticks represent the churches. There is no better place on earth for one to exert influence than in a New Testament church. A hidden holiness would be a tragedy. It has been said: "Not every Christian can build a city on a hill, but everyone can light a candle." No one can lead others closer to Christ than he himself goes.

III. The Kingdom Way of Righteousness (5:17–48)

Everywhere people were excited. A young prophet from Galilee was proclaiming that the kingdom of heaven was at hand. The Jews wanted immediately to know if he would destroy the law of Moses and the teachings of the prophets, of which they were assumed to be the guardians and interpreters. Jesus was ready to declare his position.

1. *The Kingdom and the Law* (5:17–20)

Jesus quickly revealed that he was neither a revolutionary destructionist nor a reactionary conservative, as far as Moses and the prophets were concerned. He declared that not "one jot or one tittle"—as we say, not a dot of an "i" or crossing of a "t"—of revealed truth would ever pass away.

Jesus attacked only the man-made traditions and misinterpretations of the Scriptures. He always maintained with unwavering loyalty that the law of Moses and the teachings of the prophets were indestructible. He came to fulfil them, that is, to declare the larger and more heavenly meaning within them. To fulfil them would be like completing the building of a noble cathedral that had been under construction for a long time.

The Saviour must have staggered his hearers when he said: "Except your righteousness shall exceed the righteousness of the scribes and Pharisees, ye shall in no case enter into the kingdom of heaven." The scribes and Pharisees whom Jesus denounced specialized in professing to be righteous according to the law of Moses. But theirs was a legal righteousness, a punctilious performance of the letter of the law, without the spirit of love for God and their fellow men.

2. Positive Interpretations of the Law (5:21–48)

Jesus exalted the prohibitions of the law of Moses by demanding a positive spiritual obedience motivated by love in the hidden chambers of the heart. He said one is great or small in the kingdom in proportion to his obedience to, and teaching of, the true spirit of the Law and the Prophets. Jesus gave six illustrations showing how righteousness in the kingdom of heaven exceeds the righteousness of the scribes and Pharisees.

(1) *Murder.*—The very existence of any social order is endangered by murder. If a Jew killed another, the custom was to have him arraigned before a local court of seven persons. Jesus went deeper. He forbade the willingness to kill, forbade anger in the heart, because anger is the root of which murder is the fruit.

Jesus forbade one even to use such terms of contempt as "Raca" or "fool." Kingdom men should never be contemptuous toward any man for whom Christ died. In the kingdom it is wrong to assassinate another's character, or to attack his reputation. It is not enough merely to refrain from the act of killing. If the King of love reigns in the heart, one must refrain from heart hatred, must refuse to be contemptuous toward others, must resist the temptation to assassinate another's reputation. Love in the heart is the only true guide.

Sincerity of worship is involved in such an attitude. Before worshiping, one in the kingdom should take the initiative to try to bring about a reconciliation with an offended or an offensive brother. Christians should strive to be at peace or to make peace without resorting to courts of litigation. If one does resort to the courts, he must be willing to abide by the rigorous demands of the law, for he will be compelled to pay to the last farthing assessed. One can worship but poorly unless he has adjusted properly his personal differences with others.

(2) *Adultery.*—Someone has said that "what the law sketched, Christ painted completely." That statement is especially apt regarding his interpretation of the commandment about adultery. The law of Moses said one taken in adultery should be stoned. Jesus went to the depths of it and forbade lust in the heart. Purity of life is fundamental in a social order such as Jesus envisioned for his kingdom.

The eye and the hand are the accomplices of adultery. By the use of the word translated "offend," Jesus compared them to the trigger that springs a trap on wild game. He used the dramatic metaphor of surgery of hand or eye rather than letting them lead into adultery. Avoid the one who tempts; shun the environment that allures. It is better to sacrifice anything rather than to be cast into the Gehenna of torment.

(3) *Divorce.*—A basic rock in the foundation of a perfect social order is the sanctity and permanence of the marriage vow. The Jews of Jesus' time made divorce tragically easy. The Mosaic law required at least a formal legal document, not merely an oral announcement of separation and divorce. Jesus reverted to the primal purpose of God and declared that the marriage vow is binding for life. It could be broken in life only by fornication, in which case one was as though dead to the innocent spouse. God ordained monogamy; Jesus would build a heavenly social order on it.

(4) *Truthfulness.*—Jesus said: "I am . . . the truth." He is building his kingdom on truth, and his kingdom citizens must be truthful. Speech reveals the soul. Some of the scribes and Pharisees had built up an elaborate system of nonbinding oaths and permissible lying. In the kingdom of heaven one should have such character that his word is sufficient. No oath is necessary. "Yes," and nothing more, should be inviolable truth, worthy of all acceptance.

(5) *Retaliation.*—The kingdom of heaven built on love cannot sanction revenge or retaliation for personal wrong. The writings of Moses permitted "eye for eye, tooth for tooth" (Ex. 21:24; Deut. 19:21; Lev. 24:20), to be executed by a judge in order to restrain people from overviolence. Moses did not advocate tit-for-tat retaliation.

Jesus mentioned five occasions that men were using for retaliation: assault, going into lawsuits, forceful impression into service, begging, and borrowing. Jesus was not giving rules; he was propounding principles. He was saying that the kingdom of heaven is one of love and that all hatred or retaliation or littleness of soul should be overcome by positive love. Love turns the other cheek rather than hit back; love gives the outer coat also rather than hate the man who sues for the inner garment; love goes the second mile rather than show a rancorous spirit; love gives rather than be niggardly; love lends rather than be uncharitable.

(6) *Love of enemies.*—The contrast between the righteousness in the kingdom of heaven and that of the scribes and Pharisees was climaxed by the teaching that one should love everybody, even enemies. Love counts everyone as a neighbor, even one of another race or an enemy. Jesus said pray for enemies. He knew that praying for enemies would mean that soon there would be no enemies. Love is the best revenge.

The perfect demonstration of this kingdom principle was made by the King himself when he prayed, "Father, forgive them; for they know not what they do." Such love is the essential spirit of the kingdom of heaven in action. One should earnestly desire to be as perfect in love as God is.

IV. THE KINGDOM SPIRIT OF SINCERITY (6:1-18)

In the fifth century "Saint" Simon Stylites lived thirty-seven years atop a pillar sixty feet high and three feet wide, to show his consecration (emphasis on *show*). Simon was delightfully conspicuous, even if not delightfully comfortable, parading his religion before people who gaped and marveled. He had his reward from men, not God. Doubtless his pride was as high as his pillar. He should have read the Sermon on the Mount.

Soul-deep sincerity, not religious showmanship, is the hallmark of the kingdom of heaven. "Take care not to try to demonstrate how good you are in the presence of men, in order to be seen by them. If you do, you have no reward with your Father in heaven" (Matt. 6:1).[1]

The spirit of pride is the antithesis of the spirit of the kingdom of heaven. The Pharisees sought to demonstrate their righteousness through three very frequent religious activities: almsgiving, prayer, and fasting. All were used as exhibitions of religiosity before men. The motive is what God sees.

1. Giving (6:1-4)

Giving is an acid test for pure motives. The religionists were great almsgivers, especially when witnessed by onlookers. Their motive often was to build up the reputation of being exceedingly generous. Jesus must have smiled knowingly at his disciples when he described a man who, when about to drop a coin in a beggar's cup, unloosed his bugle from his shoulder strap and tooted away to attract attention. The Master could use sanctified sarcasm!

The Pharisees in question were good actors, giving their charity with great ostentation. Jesus called them hypocrites, actors wearing masks. Since their motive was to win the praise of men, Jesus said they were paid in full and need expect no reward from God. When he spoke of not letting the left hand know what the right hand was doing, he was not advocating secrecy for secrecy's sake, but urging the

[1] From *The Gospel of Matthew*, Vol. II by William Barclay. Published 1959, The Westminster Press. Used by permission.

right motive. The word "openly" (v. 4) is not in the oldest and best manuscripts. Seeking an "open" reward was the very thing Jesus was speaking against.

2. Praying (6:5–15)

The scribes and Pharisees prayed at stated times on the clock every day wherever they were, as Moslems do today. Some of them took care to be on the street corners or in the synagogues among the throngs at the proper time to parade their prayer life. The hypocrites! They prayed long prayers, vainly repeating them by rote, believing that the more times they did so the greater was their reward.

"Enter into thy closet, and . . . pray to thy Father which is in secret," was the urgent admonition of Jesus. Prayer in public was not forbidden or discouraged. Jesus meant that public prayer should be equally as sincere as prayer in a private trysting place with God. In the parable of the importunate widow (Luke 18:1–8) Jesus commended long and persistent prayer from the heart. Those who pray in order to gain popular approval are paid in full in popular approval; they need expect no reward for their piety in the kingdom of heaven.

The heart's desire of the kingdom citizen is expressed in what we call the Lord's Prayer. It is addressed: "Our Father which art in heaven." The all-encompassing petition, "Hallowed be thy name," should be the underlying purpose of all praying, that is, the desire for the glory of God. What will hallow or glorify the name of God? "Thy kingdom come." The kingdom will come in the hearts of men if they surrender their lives to the absolute rule of Christ.

First, one's will must be surrendered if he prays sincerely, "Thy will be done in earth, as it is in heaven."

Next, God's control of all the realms of economic life, the material possessions of life, is implied in the petition, "Give us this day our daily bread."

The third request, "Forgive us our debts, as we forgive our debtors," implies that all relationships between man and man are to be subject to the authority and direction of the King.

Fourth, the realm of righteousness in Christ is to be accepted when one prays, "Lead us not into temptation, but deliver us from evil."

The additional petition does not appear in the older manuscripts: "Thine is the kingdom, and the power, and the glory, for ever." However, it is in line with the heart's desire of the kingdom citizen. The whole realm of hopes for future power and glory should be under the divine rule of the coming King. To say this Model Prayer merely by rote, as a ritual, availeth little.

3. *Fasting* (6:16-18)

"I fast twice in the week," boasted the proud Pharisee in a parable which Jesus told. It was not his fasting but his boasting that Jesus condemned. Fasting may be beneficial to health, and it certainly can be a means of self-discipline. It does not bring any spiritual blessings if it is practiced to bid for public recognition of superior piety. God knows the difference between self-discipline and self-display. Fasting, to be worthy before God, should be voluntary. All religious performance worthy of the kingdom of heaven must be motivated by inner, spiritual desire to glorify God.

V. THE KINGDOM ATTITUDE TOWARD MATERIAL THINGS (6:19-34)

A preacher closed his sermon by an appeal for scriptural giving of money. After the service a layman said: "Pastor, that was a great sermon, but I think you ruined it at the close by talking about money."

The pastor replied: "Yes, Abraham had a great experience with Melchizedek, but he ruined it by paying him tithes. Paul wrote a great treatise on the resurrection in 1 Corinthians 15, but he ruined it by saying immediately, 'Now concerning the collection . . .' Jacob at Bethel had a glorious vision of angelic hosts, but he ruined it by promising tithes to God. The Sermon on the Mount is the greatest sermon of all time, but Jesus ruined it by making over one fifth of it to refer directly to money."

Jesus knew that no man is any stronger spiritually than his attitude toward money and what money can buy. Jesus understood the vital relationship between gold and godliness. He was aware of the plague of materialism, the very antithesis of spirituality. Jesus did not discourage the making of money; he deplored the fact that some men give money the place that God should occupy in the affections.

"Lay not up for yourselves treasures upon earth, . . . but lay up for yourselves treasures in heaven." Heaven can become a celestial depository, secure and eternal. Possessions in Jesus' time often consisted of elaborate clothing, subject to moths and deterioration. Money was kept in homes, where thieves could easily dig through the soft, baked-clay bricks and steal it.

The Saviour's words have a wider application than to money alone; they apply to whatever money can buy. Jesus did not faintly condemn or forbid riches. He only taught men how to convert their temporary possessions into imperishable treasures.

GIVE AWAY

Carve your name high above shifting sand,
    Where the stedfast rocks defy decay;
But all you can hold in your cold, dead hand
    Is what you have given away.

Build your pyramids skyward, and stand
    Gazed at by millions: cultured, they say;
But all you can hold in your cold, dead hand
    Is what you have given away.

Conquest and gold and fame; Ah how grand!
King of the salon, the mart, a day—
But all you can hold in your cold, dead hand
Is what you have given away.

E. M. POTEAT, SR.

The throne of worship of a Christian's heart should be in heaven, not in a national bank. A kingdom man's deity should be Almighty God, not the almighty dollar. "Where your treasure is, there will your heart be also" (v. 21).

"The lamp of the body is the eye" (v. 22, ASV). To Orientals the eye was the window of the soul. It is a most expressive feature of the face. The "single eye" was the clear window of a godly soul; the "evil eye" was one distorted and blurred by such poison as covetousness or worldly-mindedness about things which money can buy. Such covetousness is idolatry. Money easily can become the rival of God for a man's affections. If the light of the love of God is blinded by inordinate love of money, how dense the darkness of the soul will be!

"Ye cannot serve God and mammon." Kingdom men are the bond servants of Christ, not slaves to material possessions. Money is a magnificent slave; it is a frightful and tyrannical master. "Mammon" is the Aramaic word for earthly possessions, whether good or bad. Jesus warned against slavery to mammon, because one cannot be equally loyal or obedient to two rival masters. Nothing enslaves the soul more subtly and drives God off the throne of one's affections more tragically than love of this world's goods.

"So I tell you, stop worrying about your life, as to what you will have to eat or drink, or about your body, as to what you will have to wear" (Matt. 6:25, Williams).[2] Stop being overly anxious about things which money can buy, warned

---

[2] Charles B. Williams, *The New Testament in the Language of the People* (Chicago: Moody Press, 1958). Used by permission.

Jesus. He was far from forbidding foresight such as life insurance or a savings account. He was warning against anxious worry, sleepless fretting, and agonizing fear about security in the future. Such attitudes reveal a lack of faith in the loving willingness of God to provide. Such overanxiety is a type of practical atheism.

Not to trust God is downright heathenish, for the heathen do not know a providential loving God to trust. Diligence in business and trustfulness of heart seem to be the scriptural prescription for kingdom peace and poise and power.

Jesus concluded his mighty discourse on money by the arresting summary: "Seek ye first the kingdom of God, and his righteousness; and all these things shall be added unto you." He said that wholesome food and good clothing will be added as allies to abundant, useful living, if the kingdom of heaven is put first in one's purpose. The God of the kingdom of heaven will keep him in perfect peace whose mind is fixed foremost on promoting the kingdom. Let the morrow be anxious for itself.

VI. The Kingdom Righteousness in Various Realms (7:1–23)

By the time Jesus reached this point in his sermon, the hearers doubtless were ablaze with excitement. His was relevant, vital, and dynamic preaching. He continued to discuss righteousness under the messianic rule in contrast with the lesser righteousness of the scribes and Pharisees.

1. *Judgment of Others and Self* (7:1–6)

When Jesus taught that men should not judge others with critical harshness, he did not forbid having an honest opinion about the character and conduct of another. He was condemning unkind criticism and constant faultfinding. Such an attitude will be repaid measure for measure. It is the law of the harvest; sow criticism and reap criticism.

Jesus used a typical Oriental hyperbole about this, which perhaps brought forth a hearty laugh from his hearers. He asked why one would try to remove a mote (a dust particle, a straw, a chip, a little splinter) from another's eye when there was a beam (a rafter, a joist, a log, a fence rail) in his own eye. One should clean up around his own house before he criticizes the housekeeping of others. To be hypercritical is to be hypocritical. In such action one deceives himself more than he deceives others. Love begets love, not vicious criticism.

Jesus warned against the other extreme, careless appraisal of others. A person can discriminate between people when he loves them. Christians are warned against putting sacred and holy things before those who would receive them only to defile them, like scavenger dogs would defile something very precious or like repulsive swine would defile costly pearls. Leaders should cultivate the ability to discern whether an individual is ready or unready to receive a certain truth.

2. *Prayer* (7:7-11)

It is difficult to steer wisely between censoriousness and carefulness in watching men's character. The best help is prayer. Often this is what men need most and do the poorest. The Saviour used three metaphors: ask and keep on asking; seek and keep on seeking; knock and keep on knocking. He did not encourage repetition for repetition's sake, but a soul-gripping faith that will not let go.

A loving heavenly Father will answer prayer in the best way. Even as an earthly father would not give a stone to a son asking for bread nor give a serpent to a child asking fish, so the heavenly Father will answer prayer with the gifts that are best for his children. God is too wise to answer always just as men ask, but he is too good to refuse to answer prayer.

Jesus urged his disciples to pray for the good things, the

blessings that attend righteousness in the kingdom of heaven. The Holy Spirit is the best of helps toward such praying (cf. Luke 11:13).

3. The Golden Rule (7:12)

Kingdom righteousness in relation to other people is summed up in the Golden Rule: "All things whatsoever ye would that men should do to you, do ye even so to them." This is perhaps the most widely acclaimed thing that Jesus ever said. Confucius, the Greeks, the Romans, the Buddhists, and the Jewish rabbis, had all expressed negative sentiments resembling this, but none ever stated it positively as did Jesus. One can obey the negative by doing nothing; the law of the land can compel that. Only kingdom love can motivate the positive. Love takes the initiative. This statement of Jesus is not so much a rule as a principle by which to live.

The Golden Rule can be applied in clashes of classes and clans, in settling race problems, in smoothing out domestic troubles, in solving relations between management and labor, in guiding political rivals, and in controlling business competition.

4. The Choice of Ways (7:13–14)

Success or failure in life usually depends on choices. One must choose the right Lord, the right way of happiness, the right standards of morality, the right attitude toward money, the right relations with other people, if he expects to grow and succeed in the kingdom of heaven. Jesus said one should choose the narrow gate and go with the few who are entering therein. The pathway to victorious living is found along the narrow and lonely way of obedience to Christ.

5. Genuineness of the Kingdom (7:15–23)

Anything so magnificent as the kingdom of heaven will be counterfeited. Jesus warned against insincere leaders and false messiahs. The fruits of their works reveal their nature. Whether or not they are actually in the kingdom can be detected by their words, their behavior, their temper, their influence. A rotten tree cannot produce good fruit; a polluted fountain cannot pour forth pure water.

Not everyone who makes a loud profession by saying, "Lord, Lord," is in the kingdom of heaven. True orthodoxy (straight thinking and teaching) will be accompanied by orthopraxy (straight doing). If a man have not the spirit of Christ, he is none of his.

Many will be surprised and horrified at the consummation of the kingdom when the King and Judge of all the earth will say: "I never knew you: depart from me, ye that work iniquity."

VII. THE KINGDOM CHARACTER WHICH WILL NOT COLLAPSE (7:24-27)

The crash of collapsing character is heard everywhere. Jesus came to build character that would stand any test or withstand any circumstance. He closed the Sermon on the Mount by giving a parable of two houses, one built on a rock foundation by a sensible and farseeing man, the other built on a sand foundation by a foolish and shortsighted man. The elements of wind, rain, and flood smote against both houses in fury. One stood, and the other fell, although the same forces struck both.

Just so it is today. Some characters are collapsing while others are nobly withstanding the stressful temptations of life. Is the real cause of the collapse of character found in liquor or materialism or decay of home life or laxity of law enforcement or other such reasons? These are the occasions of the collapse, like the rain and flood and wind. The fundamental cause is the poor foundation on which men are building character. Everlasting security can be had by anyone who will hear and do what Jesus taught.

VIII. CONCLUSION (7:28–29)

The principles set forth by Jesus left his hearers breathless. The disciples marveled then at his wonderful words; the world marvels today at Jesus' eternal principles for victorious living in the kingdom of heaven. The authority of heaven was and is behind him.

FOR RESEARCH AND DISCUSSION

1. Can you cite specific cases of how some people today are utilizing the plan of Jesus for happiness, and how they are succeeding?
2. How do you reconcile the two sayings of Jesus, "I am the light of the world," and, "Ye are the light of the world"?
3. Are there elemental differences between the sin of wanting to kill a man and the sin of actually killing him?
4. How is the whole Christian social order involved by the practice of remarriage after divorce?
5. Did Jesus condemn a public subscription for a new church building or condemn prayer in public?
6. What is the proper method by which a Christian can correct another's faults, without violating Jesus' command to "judge not"? (Consider Gal. 6:1.)
7. What do you think are the chief occasions of the collapse of character today, as illustrated by the rains, the floods, and the winds?
8. For further reading secure the book *Teachings of Jesus in Matthew 5–7* by Eddleman.

CHAPTER 5

I. THE KING EXERCISING AUTHORITY AND POWER (8:1 to 9:38)
1. Over Sickness (8:2–17; 9:20–22, 27–34)
2. Over Personal Affairs of Men (8:18–22; 9:9)
3. Over the Elements of Nature (8:23–27)
4. Over the Demon World (8:28–34)
5. Over Forgiveness of Sin (9:1–8)
6. Over Social Customs (9:10–13)
7. Over Religious Observances (9:14–17)
8. Over Death (9:18–26)

II. THE KING IMPARTING AUTHORITY AND POWER TO THE TWELVE (10:1–42)
1. Selecting His Co-workers (10:2–4)
2. Commissioning His Twelve Apostles (10:5–15)
3. Warning His Workers (10:16–23)
4. Encouraging His Disciples (10:24–33)
5. Challenging His Witnesses (10:34–39)
6. Identifying Himself with His Faithful Ambassadors (10:40–42)

III. THE KING DOUBTED, BLASPHEMED, AND REJECTED (11:1 to 12:50)
1. John the Baptist Doubts (11:2–15)
2. People Criticize and Reject (11:16–24)
3. Jesus Prays and Pleads (11:25–30)
4. Pharisees Accuse (12:1–45)
5. Mary Misunderstands (12:46–50)

5

The King Demonstrates His Power but Is Rejected

Matthew 8–12

CAESAR AUGUSTUS, the first Roman ruler to be called emperor, was on the throne when Jesus was born. Following the death of his uncle, Julius Caesar (44 B.C.), Augustus disposed first of Lepidus, and later of Antonius, rival claimants to the throne. Thus Augustus became the sole ruler of the Roman world.

Jesus came to be King of the kingdom of heaven. He would not conquer by force, but he had to reveal his authority and power over his rivals, the evil forces of the world. He is still in the conquest. When at last he shall have destroyed all the forces of evil, he will have fulfilled his mission as Prince of peace.

I. THE KING EXERCISING AUTHORITY AND POWER (8:1 to 9:38)

Jesus demonstrated his power over the natural and the supernatural, including the demon world. There is no other way to explain his miracles except that he came from God as an authoritative emissary.

1. Over Sickness (8:2–17; 9:20–22, 27–34)

The King has power over the bodies of men. To Jesus came a leper, victim of a most loathesome disease. In those days a leper was compelled to live outside the city walls and to cry "Unclean, unclean," when people approached within a specified distance.

This outcast and ceremonially unclean man came to Jesus with great faith, saying, "Thou canst make me clean."

Jesus touched him! Nothing could have defiled Jesus ceremonially more than this act; nothing could have delighted the untouchable leper more than to feel another man touch him sympathetically. Infinite compassion! Straightway he was healed. Jesus demonstrated the law of the kingdom of love by touching him, and the power of the King by healing him.

Jesus was able to heal, even in absentia, in response to faith. A noble and beloved centurion—commander of one hundred Roman soldiers—came to Jesus in Capernaum asking healing for his boyservant, who had suffered a stroke of palsy. This humble man said he was not fit for the Saviour to come under his roof. But his faith in the power of Jesus was so great that he asked Jesus only to speak the healing word. He knew about authority because he both obeyed it and exercised it in the army, so he asked Jesus to use his authority over sickness to heal his servant.

Jesus marveled at the centurion's faith. He said that many Gentiles with faith like this would come from the remote parts of the earth to eat at the messianic feast—that is, to share the reign of the Messiah—while some of the descendants of Abraham, Isaac, and Jacob would be cast outside in the darkness. The Jews understood the meaning, for they expected a great feast when the Messiah should come, from which they thought the Gentiles would be excluded.

The power of Jesus did not require the crowds as onlookers. His delight in relieving suffering humanity led him to cure Peter's mother-in-law from a raging fever—Luke calls it a great fever—while in the privacy of the home. Only the complete healing and restoring power of Jesus could overcome both the disease and any resulting weakness. This and other miracles attracted so much attention that by nightfall many sick and demon-possessed people were brought to Jesus.

A strange manifestation of Christ's power over sickness came when a woman with an issue of blood merely touched his garment and was healed. Jesus felt "virtue," or power, go out of him, and asked who had touched him. The woman's chronic ailment had grown worse for twelve years, yet Christ's cure was instant.

Even blindness and lack of speech were subject to the compassionate command of Jesus. He could not resist the appeals for mercy from two blind men and from a dumb man possessed with a demon. Faith in him was all he asked. People marveled to see such power, but the jealous Pharisees said it came from the prince of demons.

By such accounts, Matthew proved his point: The King of the kingdom of heaven has complete power over the bodies of men, and he will exercise that power in response to the simplest faith.

2. *Over Personal Affairs of Men* (8:18-22; 9:9)

The test of good citizenship in the kingdom of heaven is one of loyalty and obedience to the King. Two men came professing to accept his authority, yet having less than complete surrender to his lordship. One, a scribe, addressing Jesus as Teacher, impulsively said, "I will follow thee whithersoever thou goest." The other asked that, before following Jesus about the country, he might go to take care of his old father until the latter's death and burial.

The first man was the impulsive, easily influenced type. He probably was swayed by the great personality of Jesus. It may be that he was personally ambitious, thinking that Jesus would soon be on a throne—either of Israel or Rome!—and he would get an exalted position. Things looked different when Jesus revealed his own poverty—not having a roof over his head nor being as well off as the foxes or birds.

This revelation of Jesus' poverty checked the man, whether he had the shallow emotionalism of one who did not count the cost of discipleship or whether he was selfishly ambitious to be associated with the powerful miracle-worker. He apparently was not ready to accept Jesus' teaching that greatness in the kingdom of heaven is inward and not outward; it is dependent on personal righteousness and not position or possessions.

The man who wanted to wait until his father died had a divided allegiance. When Jesus said, "Follow me; and let the dead bury their dead," he did not mean that there is a conflict between faithful kingdom loyalty and filial loyalty. Each should take its proper place. However, the exalted call for allegiance to the King is superior to earthly relationships. One marvels that Christ could claim such authority over the lives and loyalties of men.

Matthew modestly inserts his own testimony about his call to full-time vocational service and his obedience to the authority of the Master. A despised tax collector for Rome seemingly was a very unlikely candidate for the ministry. But Christ, with divine authority, laid his hand upon Matthew and called him into a majestic life of service in the kingdom. Jesus looked into the character and training of this despised publican and knew he would become immortally great if his talents were dedicated to the kingdom of heaven.

Matthew did not waver when Jesus called. He arose and followed Christ as the sovereign of his life. Through the ages this same authoritative Sovereign has called his subjects away from secular pursuits into business for the King.

3. *Over the Elements of Nature* (8:23–27)

"Fear not" runs like a motif through the music of God's message to men. Fear of sickness or calamity or death can be dispelled only through faith in him who is more powerful than these enemies.

Jesus was with his disciples in a little boat crossing the

Sea of Galilee, when a terrific tempest swept down upon them. The winds were furious and the waves rolled high. The twelve were frantic with fear, and cried out, "Lord, save us: we perish!" Jesus the Creator of the winds and the waves, arose and rebuked the disciples' lack of faith. Speaking with the authority of the Master of nature, he said to the winds and waves, "Be silent, hush." Men marveled that he had power over the elements.

4. *Over the Demon World* (8:28–34)

When God incarnated himself in Jesus in an unusual manifestation of deity among men, it was natural for the god of the unseen world of evil to manifest himself also in an unusual way. There are New Testament statements which imply that Satan, the ruler of this realm of sin,—who cannot himself be all places at once—has his demons in various places, seeking to promote his evil purpose. During the life of Jesus, demons possessed men with grievous control.

Jesus manifested his power over the demons that possessed two men in the country of the Gadarenes. These men had more than some mental derangement. They were under the dominion of evil spirits. The demons recognized Jesus as their natural enemy. They knew that by his power they eventually would be overcome, therefore they asked to be sent into a large herd of hogs nearby. Jesus granted their request, and the swine ran off the precipice into the water.

Jesus considered people to be more valuable than property. By restoring these men to normal life, he demonstrated magnificently that he had power over Satan and his demons. Alas! The citizens begged Jesus to leave their countryside, evidently preferring property to people.

5. *Over Forgiveness of Sin* (9:1–8)

When Jesus spoke with authority about forgiving the sins of a paralytic who was brought to him, the scribes accused him of blasphemy. The majesty of Jesus in claiming the authority to forgive sin was overwhelming. Such authority ranked him with God. Not all sickness is the result of sin by the afflicted one, but some is. Jesus recognized sin as the cause of that man's palsy, and he spoke forgiveness before he said, "Arise, take up thy bed." The people marveled that God had given such authority and power to any one, and they glorified God.

6. Over Social Customs (9:10–13)

Few claims of Jesus infuriated the Pharisees so much as when he claimed authority over their social and religious traditions. He was in Matthew's home at a reception given in his honor. Some of Matthew's publican friends were there and also some notorious "sinners," that is, those who lived in open violation of the Jewish ceremonial law. The Pharisees—who undoubtedly stood outside—were horrified. Jesus had defied their social traditions! But he revealed the nature of his mission. He had come as the Great Physician to heal the sin-sick, not the righteous. He refuted their criticism by quoting Hosea 6:6, where God said, "I desired mercy, and not sacrifice." Jesus made goodness attractive.

7. Over Religious Observances (9:14–17)

Men are loath to accept new ideas about religious practices. When Jesus did not fast on the customary days, he was using his authority to release men from the bondage of ritual and to bring in the new spirit of the kingdom of heaven. To try to patch this new spirit on the old traditions and man-made customs of the Jews would have been like putting a new patch on an old garment, or like putting fermenting and expanding wine into old, hardened, and unelastic wineskins. The new spiritual life of the kingdom demanded new forms of expression.

8. *Over Death* (9: 18–26)

Death—cruel and inevitable death—is an enemy to God and men. "The last enemy that shall be destroyed is death" (1 Cor. 15:26). The act of raising the little daughter of the ruler of the synagogue showed the authority and power of Jesus over death itself.

This synagogue official was willing to acknowledge Jesus. With anguish in his heart he turned to the source of divine help, saying that his only daughter was at the point of death. Later, one came saying the little child was dead (Mark and Luke). The father had great faith in the power of Jesus even to raise her from the dead. On entering the house, Jesus said the little girl was not dead but sleeping, whereupon the professional mourners and hired flutists rudely laughed him to scorn. Jesus took her by the hand, and said, "Little girl, get up."

At other times the sovereign King raised from the dead a widow's son in Nain while his body was being carried to the grave, and raised Lazarus after putrefaction had set in. Never was the superiority of the kingdom of heaven over other realms more wondrously displayed than in its power over death. Never was the authority of the King more majestic.

Crowds, crowds, crowds of people! The demonstrations of the power of Jesus attracted multitudes of sick, tormented, and bewildered people who were harassed by the very things he had overcome. People are still spiritually destitute, groping, dejected, needing the reign of Christ in their hearts. Jesus saw such people as like scattered sheep or like over-ripe wheat spoiling in the fields for want of reapers. He taught his disciples to pray that his people would be good witnesses, fervent soul-winners, stouthearted missionaries, faithful reapers.

II. THE KING IMPARTING AUTHORITY AND POWER TO THE TWELVE (10:1–42)

"Then He called His twelve disciples to Him, and gave them authority over foul spirits, so that they could drive them out, and so that they could cure any disease or ailment" (10:1, Williams).[1]

1. *Selecting His Co-workers* (10:2–4)

One of the first things the President of the United States does after his election is to pick a cabinet to help him govern the nation according to his platform. Likewise, Jesus chose as his helpers twelve apostles (Greek *apostolos*, meaning messenger, or ambassador). These, his ambassadors, were to preach the principles of the kingdom of heaven and to win people to fealty to the King. The New Testament gives their names four times, with some variations, which can be accounted for easily by double names or nicknames. (An able discussion of the four lists is given in Robertson's *A Harmony of the Gospels*, pp. 271–273.)

The men whom Jesus chose had little wealth, little formal higher education, position, or prestige. No other group of this size ever made such a profound impact upon the world. Winston Churchill's famous words have been aptly applied: "Never . . . was so much owed by so many to so few." Later, these men had a profound and soul-deep conviction that Christ had risen from the dead and was the King of the kingdom of heaven. This conviction impelled them in their ongoing mission. One shudders to think what would have become of the Christian movement if they had failed Christ.

2. *Commissioning His Twelve Apostles* (10:5–15)

With imperial command Jesus sent out his twelve ambas-

---

[1] Charles B. Williams, *The New Testament in the Language of the People*. (Chicago: Moody Press, 1958). Used by permission.

sadors into Galilee on urgent kingdom business. They were told to begin with "the lost sheep of the house of Israel," since they were not yet prepared for Gentile conquest. They were to preach that the kingdom of heaven was at hand, thus echoing the theme of Jesus' preaching (Matt. 4:17).

In order to prove that their authority was from the King, they were given the King's powers: "Heal the sick, raise the dead, cleanse the lepers, cast out demons" (10:8, ASV). They were told to dispense these heavenly powers freely in order to relieve souls and bodies from the despotism of Satan.

"Freely give" did not mean they should not receive compensation from those among whom they worked. They were told not to take along any money for trading, nor clothing for social purposes, nor food for sustenance. They were not to expect charity, but a well-earned remuneration, sufficient to relieve them from all anxiety. Instruction to the apostles said, "Freely give"; instructions to those to whom the apostles ministered said, "The workman is worthy of his meat."

The apostles were to be gracious guests, seeking for homes where they were wanted, not seeking homes because they were more luxurious. Guests were to be courteous, greeting the host with *Shalom,* the benediction of peace, health, prosperity, and happiness.

Jesus told his messengers to shake the dust off their feet— as Jews did when leaving Gentile country—if hospitality was refused. Since time was important, the King's ambassadors were to go where opportunities for results were best. The responsibility for failure was not upon the apostles but upon any hearers who refused the tidings from the King. Sodom and Gomorrah, emblems of wickedness and sensuality, had been given no such opportunities to hear the gospel as had the cities of Galilee; therefore, they would have no such severe judgment as the cities which refused to hear the apostles.

3. *Warning His Workers* (10:16–23)

History has fulfilled the warning of Jesus to his apostles and his ambassadors of future generations about the hatreds and persecutions they would suffer from the men of the world. "Beware of men," said he.

Worldly hearts and the hearts where Christ reigns are as different as ravening wolves and harmless sheep. One should face the world with the wisdom, caution, and self-protecting sagacity of a serpent as well as with the harmlessness, inoffensiveness, and gentleness of a dove. These characteristics are parallel, like the rails of a railroad track. Serpentlike sharpness alone might lead to unworthy scheming; dovelike simplicity alone might lead to gullibility. Beware of men, especially unregenerate men!

When he was tried and crucified at the hands of Jewish and Roman courts, Jesus himself experienced the indignities against which he had warned. For many centuries his followers have been persecuted by government decrees. Until Roger Williams of Providence Plantations, Rhode Island, in 1636, decreed the right for one to worship God or not to worship according to the dictates of his conscience, there was no government in the world's history that had granted religious liberty as the inalienable right of every individual.

While under persecution, true Christians have borne some of their noblest witnesses for Christ. The Spirit of the Father tells the trusting soul how to testify while in peril of dungeon, fire, or sword.

Jesus forewarned that loyalty to the kingdom or rebellion against it would divide families, brother from brother, parents from children. Perseverance while under persecution is a mighty evidence of true salvation, for "he that endureth to the end shall be saved."

However, Jesus did not teach that one is to invite martyrdom foolishly. "But when they persecute you in this city,

flee ye into another." The Saviour promised that he himself
would follow them throughout the cities of Israel.

4. *Encouraging His Disciples* (10:24-33)

The greatest glory for a disciple of Christ is to be like his
Lord. Jesus forewarned and forearmed the twelve by saying
they would suffer as he suffered. They were to "fear not"
four things: First, fear not being called reproachful, infamous, contemptuous names. Second, fear not failure; the kingdom message would be proclaimed publicly and boldly.
Third, fear not those persecutors who could kill only the body;
fear only God's displeasure at sin. One who chooses sin will
have both body and soul cast into the hell (*gehenna*) of
separation from God with its torment. Fourth, fear not that
God will forsake his own while in persecution. God cares
even for the common sparrow that falls; even the hairs of
one's head are numbered.

The judgment of men before whom Christ's followers will
be brought is not nearly so important as the judgment of the
King of glory. The greatest glory for a saint in the judgment
will be to be recognized and rewarded by the King. To
confess him on earth—that is, to witness for him by righteous
living, by soul-winning, by acknowledging him when in
temptation or persecution—will bring his rewarding recognition in that day. What shame could equal that of being
denied by him before the Father in heaven?

5. *Challenging His Witnesses* (10:34-39)

One of the best ways to challenge soldiers to loyalty and
bravery in warfare is to tell about the hardships and terrors
of the campaign; that is also one of the best ways to screen
out the cowards and disloyal ones. Winston Churchill promised blood and sweat and tears, but victory and glory.
Napoleon pictured the rigors of crossing the Alps, but said,
"Over the Alps lies Italy."

Jesus was always realistic and challenging. He said loyalty to him would bring warfare and divisions even between the nearest of kin. Jesus did not believe in peace at the price of disloyalty and compromise. He challenged his disciples to heroic cross-bearing, that is, to be willing to submit to suffering or death for his sake. He gave one of his paradoxical truths: "He that findeth his life shall lose it: and he that loseth his life for my sake shall find it."

He who loses the lower order of life, the selfish life, shall find in Christ the higher spiritual life. When one forgets his own life in noble adventure of faith and service, he begins to experience the abundant life which Jesus gives.

The predictions about wars, hatreds, and divisions may have shocked the twelve, for they looked for a Messiah to usher in a reign of peace. They did not realize that there must first be the reign of righteousness before there can be the reign of peace.

6. Identifying Himself with His Faithful Ambassadors (10:40-42)

Those who receive and entertain an ambassador of the King are receiving the King himself. The humble and obscure who can give a missionary of Christ only a cup of cold water will be exalted by the King. Blessed are those who offer their homes and helpfulness to Christ's preachers, evangelists, missionaries, and other witnesses. Truly they are "fellowhelpers to the truth" (3 John 8).

III. THE KING DOUBTED, BLASPHEMED, AND REJECTED (11:1 to 12:50)

"And when Jesus had finished instructing his twelve disciples, he went on from there to teach and preach in their cities" (11:1, RSV). Alas, alas! When he proclaimed his kingdom to the people he met doubt, suspicion, criticism, unbelief, blasphemy, and rejection.[2]

1. John the Baptist Doubts (11:2–15)

How amazing! John the Baptist doubted—this John who saw the Holy Spirit like a dove descend out of heaven, this same John who had said, "Behold the Lamb of God!" He sent from his prison at Machaerus asking, "Art thou he that should come, or do we look for another?" John was languishing in prison, inactive and weary in a very hot climate. He had been accustomed to the freshness of open air and the excitement of preaching to great crowds. He was despondent, discouraged, despairing. Perhaps he wondered why God did not intervene to set him free.

Jesus responded by referring to his miracles on the blind, lame, leprous, deaf, and dead. John knew Isaiah 35:5–6, where these miracles were foretold. Jesus told him that the poor were having the good news of the gospel preached to them, as prophesied in Isaiah 61:1–3.

Jesus said there was none greater than John born of woman, referring to John's exalted privilege in the kingdom. Yet John did not live long enough to enter into the full knowledge of the kingdom involving the crucifixion, resurrection, and the church. Individuals who would later enter into these higher realms of knowledge and faith would be greater than John, said Jesus.

Dr. John A. Broadus described John's position as like a landing on a stairway. John the Baptist was above those who had preceded him, but below those who should live to see the kingdom advanced by the life, death, and resurrection

[2] From *The Gospel of Matthew*, Vol. II by William Barclay. Published 1959, The Westminster Press. Used by permission.

of the King.[3] John was the Elijah prophesied in Malachi
4:5, whom the Jews expected to precede the Messiah.

2. People Criticize and Reject (11:16–24)

The perversity of human hearts amazed Jesus. They rejected both John and himself. Men said austere John had
a demon; they said the warmly gracious Jesus was a glutton
and wine drinker, a friend of publicans and sinners. Jesus
condemned the cities such as Chorazin, Bethsaida, and
Capernaum, where the people would not repent and believe even though he had done many mighty works in those
places. Sodom and Tyre and Sidon were morally worse,
perhaps, but their opportunities for hearing the gospel were
not so great as those of the Galilean cities; therefore, their
responsibilities were not so great. The people of Galilee
would be more guilty in the judgment than Sodom.

3. Jesus Prays and Pleads (11:25–30)

Jesus prayed with tender compassion for those who reviled him and pleaded with yearning love with those who
rejected him. He thanked God that the secrets of the kingdom of heaven can be understood by the humble and childlike, even though they are poorly understood by the
worldly wise and the intellectually proud.

The throb of Christ's heart can be sensed as one reads
how he pleaded with burdened souls: "Come unto me, all ye
that labour and are heavy laden, and I will give you rest.
Take my yoke upon you, and learn of me; for I am meek
and lowly in heart: and ye shall find rest unto your souls."
To take his yoke means to enter his school and become a
learner in the way of superior, heavenly living. One can
scarcely keep back the tears while reading that tender-
hearted appeal.

[3] *An American Commentary on the New Testament* (Philadelphia:
The American Baptist Publication Society, 1886), I. 241.

4. *Pharisees Accuse* (12:1–45)

One of the chief reasons why the Pharisees wanted to kill Jesus was that he renounced the traditions which various rabbis had attached to the law of Moses. There were more than sixteen hundred such regulations, not a part of the inspired law. Often these rabbinical rules ran to the ridiculous. For example, one rule said that to eat an egg laid on the sabbath was unlawful. Another added that the egg could be eaten if the hen was killed for laying it. One said with gravity that it was unlawful for a woman to look into a mirror on the sabbath, for fear she might see a gray hair and be tempted to pull it out.

With this background, no wonder the orthodox Jewish leaders thought that the disciples of Jesus sinned when they went through a grain field on the sabbath, pulled a bit of wheat or barley, rubbed out the kernels, threw away the husks, and ate the grain. Lo, that was reaping, threshing, winnowing, and preparing meals!

Jesus defended the twelve by reminding the critics about the time that David was hungry and was given the shewbread from the tabernacle (1 Sam. 21:3–6) because of his need. Next, Jesus spoke of the extra work imposed upon the priests in the Temple on the sabbath when they prepared and offered the animal sacrifices on the altar (Num. 28:9), but were guiltless because God commanded it.

Jesus always stood squarely with Moses, but he denied the authority of the enslaving interpretations which had been made through the ages by different rabbis. Jesus continued, "But I tell you, there is something greater than the temple here!" (Matt. 12:6, Williams).[4] He quoted from one of their prophets, "For I desired mercy, and not sacrifice" (Hos.

---

[4] Charles B. Williams, *The New Testament in the Language of the People* (Chicago: Moody Press, 1958). Used by permission.

6:6) and stated that the King was Lord of the sabbath. This claim further infuriated the Pharisees.

When the critics of Jesus saw him on the sabbath in a synagogue where there was a man with a withered hand, they knew what he was likely to do. They were not there by accident, but to spy on him. When they asked if it was lawful to heal on the sabbath, Jesus countered by asking if it was lawful to do good on the sabbath. Their law allowed them to pull a sheep out of a ditch on the sabbath, but they looked with horror at healing a man, where there was no danger of loss of life. With Christ mercy was always superior to ceremony, and people were always more important than rules. He told the man to stretch forth his hand—something he could not have done except for the power of Jesus.

This healing on the sabbath was too much for the resolute Pharisees. They decided that the only way to preserve their traditions would be to put Jesus to death. The Saviour's time for full-scale proclamation of his messianic role had not come; he prudently withdrew to escape their hostility.

However, Jesus never ceased to heal and to bless those who came to him. Matthew quotes from Isaiah 42:1–4 to reveal that the King of kings came for a benevolent and peaceful role, rather than for a militaristic conquest, as was expected by the Jews. The "bruised reed" would not be broken; "smoking flax" would be fanned into a flame instead of quenched.

Defeated publicly in a controversy, the opponents of Jesus were reduced to calling names! They said that Jesus was under the power of Beelzebub, the prince of demons, because he cured a demon-possessed man who was also blind and dumb. With unanswerable logic Jesus exposed the absurdity of their accusation. He said that if Satan were working against Satan, then Satan would soon fall. If Jesus was casting out demons by the Spirit of God, then the kingdom of God was among them. He was victoriously entering the house of the strong man, Satan, curbing his power for evil, and spoiling his diabolic work. The Pharisees were infuriated unto blasphemy.

Blasphemy against the Holy Spirit is called the "unpardonable sin." The word "blasphemy" means to speak in an irreverent, profane, and malignant manner against God. The Pharisees did this against the Holy Spirit of God when they said: "This fellow doth not cast out devils, but by Beelzebub the prince of the devils" (12:24). Jesus said to them: "Blasphemy against the Holy Ghost shall not be forgiven unto men . . . neither in this world, neither in the world to come" (31–32). This is the unpardonable sin. Dr. A. T. Robertson says in discussing this passage:

What is the blasphemy against the Holy Spirit? These Pharisees had already committed it. They had attributed the works of the Holy Spirit by whose power Jesus wrought his miracles (12:28) to the devil. That sin was without excuse and would not be forgiven in their age or in the coming one (12:32). People often ask if they can commit the unpardonable sin. Probably some do who ridicule the manifest work of God's Spirit in men's lives and attribute the Spirit's work to the devil.[4]

Many devout Bible students believe that the sin that may not be forgiven is deliberate, persistent unbelief; it is refusing to accept Jesus Christ as Saviour and Lord and refusing to acknowledge the Holy Spirit as the spirit of God who alone can convict of sin and lead men to repentance and faith. The interpretation of the unpardonable sin as mentioned in this passage is given by Dr. John A. Broadus, as follows:

Their charge of league with Beelzebul . . . was a blasphemy against the Holy Spirit . . . was a malignant insult to God. . . . The conditions, then, under which this unpardonable sin of blasphemy against the Spirit of God is committed, are (1) that there shall be a work manifestly supernatural, unmistakably the work

---

[4] *Word Pictures in the New Testament* (Nashville: Broadman Press, 1930), I, 96–97.

of God and not of man, and (2) that one shall, in determined and malignant opposition, insultingly ascribe to Satan this which he knows to be the work of God. . . . And the familiar idea of "sinning away one's day of grace" ought not to be confounded with the blasphemy here spoken of.[5]

Opposition mounted. The scribes and Pharisees asked Jesus for a sign. Jews then were expecting the Messiah to show himself with many signs of miraculous wonder. Jesus promised the supreme sign, resurrection from the dead. He promised to rise from the heart of the earth as Jonah came forth after three days within the great sea-creature (Jonah 1:17).

The King of the kingdom of heaven is much greater than Jonah, yet the people of Ninevah repented at Jonah's preaching. Likewise the Gentile queen of Sheba came from afar to see Solomon (1 Kings 10:1–10). It enraged the Pharisees for Jesus to say that he was greater than Jonah or Solomon, and it infuriated them further to be compared disadvantageously with the Gentiles.

Jesus warned his hearers about the desperate danger of an empty heart. Reformation without regeneration is often followed by disastrous reaction. The unclean spirit of idolaltry had been driven out of Jewish life by the Babylonian captivity, and other demonlike traits had been dispelled by the Old Testament prophets. Jesus knew that the vacant places should be filled up with loyalty to the King of the kingdom of heaven.

Jesus told a parable about an unclean spirit, driven out of a house, who returned to the "swept and garnished" house and brought with him seven other spirits worse than himself. "Seven spirits" had come into Jewish life—spirits such as pride, hypocrisy, unbelief, blasphemy against the Holy Spirit, rejection of the Messiah, plotting to kill Jesus, and refusal to be moved by the love of God.

---

[5] *Ibid.*, p. 272.

5. *Mary Misunderstands* (12:46–50)

Even his mother and his brothers wanted Jesus to leave the crowds. Perhaps they shared the opinion of the friends who thought Jesus was "beside himself" (Mark 3: 21). How could Mary misunderstand, when she knew the heavenly manifestations that had attended him from his birth? Jesus no doubt appreciated her loving concern, but he could not permit interference with his ministry of proclaiming the kingdom. He declared that those who accept the rule of heaven in their lives are his spiritual brothers and sisters and mother. With him, righteousness was, and is, the basis of spiritual kinship, and the heavenly Father was esteemed even above his mother.

FOR RESEARCH AND DISCUSSION

1. Were there any limitations to the power of Christ? If so, what?
2. Why do Christians today not have healing powers such as Jesus had?
3. In what ways are Christians persecuted in the present time?
4. What various things are implied in the command to confess Christ before men?

CHAPTER 6

I. EXPLANATION OF THE KINGDOM BY PARABLES (13:1–52)

1. Sower and Soils: Various Receptions by the People (13:3–23)
2. Tares: Problem of Good and Evil (13:24–30, 36–43)
3. Mustard Seed: Small Beginning but Unlimited Growth (13:31–32)
4. Leaven: Spiritual Infiltration (13:33–35)
5. Hidden Treasure: Incomparable Value (13:44)
6. Pearl of Great Price: Ultimate of Man's Soul-Satisfaction (13:45–46)
7. Dragnet: Final Separation of the Righteous and Wicked (13:47–50)

II. WITHDRAWAL FROM KINGDOM ENEMIES: TRAINING KINGDOM DISCIPLES (13:53 to 16:12)

1. The King's Forerunner Beheaded (14:1–12)
2. Feeding Five Thousand (14:13–21)
3. Walking on Water (14:22–36)
4. Disregarding Traditional Religion (15:1–20)
5. Withdrawing into Gentile Territory (15:21–28)
6. Healing Many and Again Feeding the Multitudes (15:29–39)
7. Warning the Twelve (16:1–12)

III. ANNOUNCEMENT OF THE ESTABLISHMENT OF THE CHURCH (16:13–20)

1. The King's Deity (16:13–16)
2. Planning to Build His Church (16:17–18)
3. Purpose of His Church (16:19–20)

IV. REDEMPTIVE PLAN AND COST OF DISCIPLESHIP (16:21–28)

1. Redemption Through Crucifixion and Resurrection of the King (16:21)
2. Peter Rebuked by the King (16:22–23)
3. Discipleship Through Cross-bearing (16:24–26)
4. Rewards for Cross-bearing and Obedience (16:27–28)

6

The King Explains His Kingdom and Announces His Program

Matthew 13–16

ONLY heaven could have produced such a teacher as Jesus. He taught by the heavenly example of a sinless life; he taught by doing heavenly works; he taught with the heavenly truths that he uttered. One of his intriguing and effective methods in teaching was the use of parables. There are more than fifty of his parables in the Gospels. They explain in clear pictures the nature of the kingdom.

I. EXPLANATION OF THE KINGDOM BY PARABLES (13:1–52)

When Jesus saw that he was being misunderstood, misinterpreted, and rejected by the Jewish people, he turned aside from the populace to devote himself to teaching his disciples some intensive and fundamental truths about the kingdom of heaven. He left the synagogues and went into the open spaces. Even so, multitudes followed him.

The Master's picturesque pulpit was a swaying boat at the seashore, as he told meaningful parables to expound the eternal truths of the kingdom he had come to establish. Like the skilled teacher he was, Jesus drew his illustrations from things familiar to his hearers—home, farm, sea.

1. *Sower and Soils: Various Receptions by the People* (13:3–23)

The parable about the four soils might be called the parable of listening ears and receptive hearts. Jesus was telling

75

about how truth gets or fails to get into men's hearts. Possibly he pointed to a farmer at work and said, "Look at that man sowing seed."

Some of the seed inevitably would be blown by the winds onto the hard path. The birds would have a picnic snatching them away. This part of the parable illustrates preaching to those who are prejudiced or hardened in indifference. Satan snatches away the truth from them like birds pecking seed from the roadside. The unbelieving Pharisees were like this type of soil.

Other seed fell into thin soil that barely covered the under layer of limestone rock. These seed germinated quickly, but as quickly withered for want of depth. Many hearts are like the shallow soil—being impulsive, superficial, given to following the crowd and doing what is popular at the time. They do not have enough depth of character to meet the high demands of sustained consecration to Christ.

The third type of soil was thorny and so full of weeds that fruitfulness was impossible. The church rolls carry names of many people of this type—people who permit the love of money or love of pleasure to keep their lives from being fruitful for God. The fourth type of soil was deep, moist, rich, like hearts ready to receive the gospel, to live the truth, and to bear the fruit of righteousness. This parable warns hearers to listen and encourages them to give allegiance to Christ the King.

"Why do you speak in parables?" asked the disciples. Jesus had evidently changed to this method of teaching because of the hostility of the Jews and because of their erroneous ideas about how the messianic kingdom was to come. Parables were used to make the truth clearer to those who would receive it. At the same time, the story veiled the truth from those who would deliberately reject it. Jesus wanted his disciples to understand him, yet he wanted to speak so those who were malignantly disposed toward him would hear only stories—for which they themselves would supply the application. Those who had some willingness to understand would get more light; those who wilfully misunderstood would be plunged into greater darkness. "The mysteries of the kingdom" were like the knowledge imparted only to those who have been initiated into a secret order. The uninitiated grow dull of ears.

The disciples were highly favored to hear the truths of the kingdom explained, whereas the prophets of old had been able to see these truths only through the misty visions of prophecy.

2. Tares: Problem of Good and Evil (13:24-30, 36-43)

The Jews expected the coming Messiah to wipe out all evil ones and all enemies, as the aggressor kings of warring nations did their foes. Not so with Jesus. In the parable of the tares, or darnel, he described the works of the devil as being like noxious weeds sown by an enemy in a man's good wheat field. The enemy was Satan, always working insidiously on God's territory in an effort to destroy Christ's work. The wheat and tares were like men of the kingdom of heaven and men of the devil's kingdom all living together. The angels—ministering spirits doing the bidding of God— will have the responsibility of separating all men into two classes, the saved and the lost. The unrighteous will be cast into the fiery furnace of rebellion and agony. The righteous will shine for eternity, as promised in Daniel 12:3.

3. Mustard Seed: Small Beginning but Unlimited Growth (13:31-32)

The remarkable growth of the Christian movement was predicted in the parable of the mustard seed. The kingdom of heaven does not come by "observation," (Luke 17:20) that is "with signs to be observed" (RSV). It had a small beginning, like a mustard seed—only a few score persons before

Pentecost. The Christian faith is reported now to have between eight and nine hundred million adherents, about one-third of the world's population.

Adoniram Judson, laboring seven years in India before he had a single convert, could yet affirm, "The prospects are as bright as the promises of God."

4. *Leaven: Spiritual Infiltration* (13:33-35)

The kingdom of heaven grows "not by might nor by power," as the Jews expected, but by the Spirit of God, using the influence of Christians to win others. The parable about the leaven teaches this truth. The evident meaning is that, as the small bit of leaven infiltrates into the large amount of meal, so a few Christians would influence others on a world-wide scale.

Someone has said the early Christians won so many converts in the Roman Empire because they outloved others, outlived others, and outdied others. Genuine spirituality is the most winsome and one of the most contagious influences on earth.

5. *Hidden Treasure: Incomparable Value* (13:44)

Since ancient people had no banks, they often hid their treasures in the ground for safety. Jesus said the kingdom of heaven was like a treasure found in a field, one of immeasurable and incomparable value. There is no sacrifice which a man should hesitate to make in order to have it. The sharp practice of the man in hiding the treasure and then buying the field is not the point of the parable. The point is that men should appraise and appreciate the blessings of the kingdom. One should "sell all he hath" to obtain it. Are all of earth's praise, popularity, pleasures and possessions combined worth as much as eternal life in the kingdom? "What shall a man give in exchange for his soul?" (Matt. 16:26).

6. *Pearl of Great Price: Ultimate of Man's Soul-Satisfaction* (13:45–46)

If Jesus were giving the parable of the pearl of great price today he possibly would tell of a diamond merchant finding the Cullinan diamond—the largest owned by British royalty—and selling all his other diamonds to get the money to buy the famous one.

In life's experiences, one man is suddenly confronted with Christ and is challenged to surrender to the heavenly reign, while some other thoughtful man may seek for years to find his soul's satisfaction. In either case the kingdom is a spiritual treasure of supreme worth.

7. *Dragnet: Final Separation of the Righteous and Wicked* (13:47–50)

Jesus used fishing as a point of contact in teaching his disciples because many were fishermen. He spoke of a dragnet, or seine, hauling in many fish, which were separated, the good from the inedible ones. He was illustrating much the same truth as in the parable of the tares. He meant that his disciples in the kingdom are to cast the evangelistic net now, and at the end of the world the final separation will be made by the angelic ministers of God. Both the righteous and the wicked will be sent to their appointed destinations.

II. WITHDRAWAL FROM KINGDOM ENEMIES: TRAINING KINGDOM DISCIPLES (13:53 to 16:12)

Jesus went back to the synagogue, probably at Nazareth. But his own people doubted him, questioned about him, were hostile to him. He understood that no prophet is likely to be honored in his own country as much as in some faraway place. The unbelief of the people kept him from doing many mighty works in the Nazareth area.

Jesus was sensible and prudent. He retired to a thinly populated area northeast of the Sea of Galilee, a region ruled by Philip, the tetrarch. John the Baptist had been murdered by Herod Antipas; the crowds were growing fanatical about making Jesus a king to overthrow Rome; the disciples needed rest. Therefore, Jesus made a series of withdrawals, during which he taught his disciples many essential kingdom truths.

1. *The King's Forerunner Beheaded* (14:1–12)

The tragic death of John the Baptist is a sordid story of the infamy of Herod Antipas. He was the son of the Herod who had the babies killed at Bethlehem. Antipas married Herodias, his brother's wife, and John had the moral courage to denounce the union.

The story Matthew tells involves the vicious desire of Herodias for revenge, the lust-provoking dance of the daughter of Herodias, Herod's rash promise and moral cowardice, and the beheading of the noble servant of God. When Herod heard of the mighty works of Jesus, he trembled like a coward, for he feared that Jesus was John come back to life again. "Conscience does make cowards of us all," said Shakespeare.

2. *Feeding Five Thousand* (14:13–21)

Jesus wanted to go with his disciples to a quiet resting place, but multitudes thronged after him. Hungry, sick, and scattered people like these throngs simply wrung his heart. He healed many. He taught the multitudes much about his kingdom.

The day declined, and eating time was passed. When the disciples wanted to send the multitudes away, Jesus said to give them food. He took five little barley loaves—the coarse bread eaten by poorer people—and two little fish, and fed five thousand men plus the women and children present.

He multiplied the food by distinctly supernatural power. The miracle demonstrated the creative power of Jesus in the natural world. Twelve baskets full of the overabundance were saved, illustrating the amazing abundance of the overflowing grace of God in Christ.

Later, the people wanted to make Jesus king, for they saw that he could feed the nation and the army by miraculous power (John 6:15). But when Jesus began to teach that he himself was the Bread of life, that his flesh and blood were the true food and drink in his kingdom, and when the people saw that he did not intend to become a political or military ruler, multitudes turned away in disappointment (John 6:66).

3. *Walking on Water* (14:22–36)

The Sea of Galilee is usually a lovely little sheet of water, about thirteen miles long and seven wide, its surface some 600 feet below the level of the Mediterranean Sea. Sudden winds sometimes howl down and lash the lake into a boiling fury. This happened when Jesus sent the twelve across the lake toward Capernaum, while he dispersed the crowds after feeding the five thousand.

Meanwhile, Jesus went apart to pray. The frenzied fanaticism of those who wanted to make him king was the same type of temptation that he had faced when Satan in the wilderness offered him all the kingdoms of the world. Nothing helps in temptation like prayer.

Sometime between three and six in the morning the twelve were struggling at the oars against the storm that had descended on the Sea of Galilee. Knowing their distress, Jesus walked on the water to overtake them, another striking miracle. Jesus said, "Have courage; don't fear; it is I."

Peter was so overjoyed at seeing Jesus walking on the water that he impulsively asked the Master to enable him to walk on the water also. Christ honored his faith, and Peter did nobly until he took his eyes off Jesus and looked at the storm. When he began to sink, the only thing that saved him was a look at Jesus and a cry of faith.

This miracle was another lesson to the twelve. It taught the disciples that faith is vital in the kingdom, and it showed how doubt always brings disaster. They learned afresh that Jesus is the Son of God, and the King of all nature.

4. *Disregarding Traditional Religion* (15:1–20)

Like a head-on collision of two locomotives was the next clash with the hostile group of Jewish leaders who had banded together to oppose Jesus. Jews from Jerusalem came asking Jesus why his disciples disregarded the oral tradition of their elders by eating without the ceremonial washing of their hands. Generations of rabbis had handed down a vast volume of petty oral prohibitions about ceremonial uncleanness and many laws about hand-washing before meals. Two systems of religion were colliding, the ceremonial versus the spiritual, the rabbinical versus the Mosaic, the religion of the outside versus religion of the heart.

Jesus countered the question of his opponents by showing how their traditional law sometimes made them disobedient to God's law. He referred to the fifth commandment: "Honour thy father and mother." The oral law said that if a son for any reason, even in haste or anger, said he would not give any of his property to support his father or his mother but that he was giving it to God, his words constituted an eternal and irrevocable vow to God. This oral law said he would be justified in letting his parents starve rather than break his vow by helping them in their need. "Hypocrites!" charged Jesus. He quoted Isaiah, showing that their traditions were vain and their hearts far from God.

Jesus took this opportunity to emphasize the inwardness of the kingdom of heaven. What matters is what is in the heart, not what is in the digestive tract. What goes into the mouth, even by way of unwashed hands, does not defile morally; moral defilement comes out of the heart by way of the mouth. The Teacher showed that the sixth, seventh, eighth, and ninth commandments are broken first in the heart, before the overt acts of murder, adultery, fornication, theft, false witness, or railing.

The clash of ideologies over ceremonialism was one of the most significant religious debates in all history. "Let them alone," said Jesus, pronouncing drastic judgment, "They be blind leaders of the blind."

5. *Withdrawing into Gentile Territory* (15:21-28)

Jesus wished to get away from the Pharisees. He also wanted to avoid Herod's jealousy and to escape the unpredictable conduct of the fanatical crowds. He needed rest; his disciples needed the opportunity to be alone with him. So he went to the mountainous regions about Tyre and Sidon in Phoenicia.

A devoted Gentile mother who had great faith in Jesus came seeking his healing grace for her demon-possessed daughter. She evidently was a God-fearing Gentile. Jesus tested her faith by not answering her loud cries at first, and then later by telling her that the meat was for "the children" —the Jews—and not for the "little dogs under the table" (as his words literally mean). Perhaps Jesus smiled broadly and his eyes twinkled when he said this. Her clever and witty reply reflects the good humor in which Jesus must have said what he did. He would never have spoken disrespectfully to this good woman; he was such a gentleman!

When Jesus had commended the woman's faith and healed her daughter, he left this Gentile country. He could not afford yet to go into any extensive healing of the Gentiles; if he had, then the masses of the Jews would have been irrevocably alienated. His mission was to be first to "the lost sheep of the house of Israel."

6. *Healing Many and Again Feeding the Multitudes* (15:29–39)

Seeking to stay out of the territory of Herod Antipas, Jesus went into Decapolis, a region where the Greeks had established the "Ten Cities," of which nine were east of the Jordan and the Sea of Galilee. Multitudes followed him. His miracles had brought him to the peak of his popularity. Needy people thronged him—the sick, the dumb, the blind, the crippled, the weary and heavy laden.

Again Jesus fed a multitude who followed him—this time four thousand—by multiplying seven loaves and a few fish. Seven baskets were filled with the overabundance, one basket for each of the little loaves with which Jesus began. The same lessons were taught as when he fed the five thousand. The God of Israel was glorified, and his fame was spread abroad among the Greeks, Romans, and mixed nationalities represented in the population of that area.

7. *Warning the Twelve* (16:1–12)

The Sadducees and the Pharisees, usually bitter opponents, joined together to test Jesus. The Sadducees held that the written law alone was binding. They did not believe in the immortality of the soul or the future life. For them to join with the Pharisees, their bitter opponents, was a dangerous indication of growing opposition to Jesus. These determined critics asked Jesus for a sign from heaven. Perhaps they wanted something like a voice out of the skies or fire out of heaven such as Elijah had called down.

Jesus knew that he was doing signs which proved that he was the King of the kingdom of heaven when he was doing his mighty works of mercy to suffering humanity. The Pharisees and Sadducees knew the signs of the weather, but they did not know the signs of the kingdom of heaven. As he had done before (12:39), Jesus promised only the sign of Jonah.

The Lord moved on across the lake. The twelve either forgot to prepare their lunch, or they left it behind. Jesus took this as an occasion for warning against the skepticism and intellectual pride and political policies of the Sadducees as well as against the hypocrisy and false religious views of the Pharisees. The disciples were so hungry and so dull that they could not interpret the metaphor when Jesus warned against "the leaven of the Pharisees and of the Sadducees."

III. ANOUNCEMENT OF THE ESTABLISHMENT OF THE CHURCH (16:13–20)

Every good teacher holds examinations periodically. After some months of intense instruction, Jesus held his examination. He was near Caesarea Philippi, a city about twenty-five miles from the Sea of Galilee and in sight of snow-capped Mount Hermon. There Herod the Great had built a large marble fortress in honor of Augustus. It was built near a center where the Greek god Pan was venerated. Philip had enlarged the city and called it Caesarca Philippi.

Thus Jesus brought the twelve to an environment where a Greek god and a Roman emperor had been worshiped, and there questioned them about their belief in him. The passage telling about the examination and the instruction which followed (Matt. 16:13–28) is full of basic and exalted Christian doctrine.

1. *The King's Deity* (16:13–16)

The first examination question was, "Whom do men say that I . . . am?" The first lesson in understanding the mysteries of the kingdom of heaven is to understand the King, who he is and what his nature is.

The multitudes had varied opinions. Some thought, as did Herod Antipas, that Jesus was John the Baptist. Others imagined that he was the fulfilment of Malachi's prophecy (Mal. 4:5) about Elijah. Some guessed that he was Jeremiah, whom they believed would return to the earth again.

Simon Peter, speaking for the twelve, made a perfect grade on the examination: "Thou art the Christ, the Son of the living God." The deity of Christ is the chief cornerstone of Christian doctrine. When Peter confessed belief in his deity, Jesus burst out in joyous satisfaction. He knew that at last his twelve had the proper belief and attitude toward him.

Foreseeing his early death, Jesus desired with all his heart to have some who understood about the kingdom and believed him to be the divine King. Jesus exclaimed that Peter was a happy and fortunate man, for no flesh and blood (no mere man) could have revealed this truth to him, rather, the Father in heaven.

2. Planning to Build His Church (16:17–18)

Jesus used picturesque language, even resorting to a play on words. He said: "Thou art Peter [Greek, *Petros*], and upon this rock [Greek, *petra*] I will build my church." What did he mean?

Devout scholars differ in their understanding of the passage. Several interpretations are held among conservative Southern Baptists. Some interpret the passage to say that Jesus is the rock on which his church is being built. Peter himself later wrote of Jesus as the "chief corner stone" (1 Peter 2:6). Paul wrote: "For other foundation can no man lay than that is laid, which is Jesus Christ" (1 Cor. 3:11).

Other interpreters have said that the church is built on Peter's confession, or on a faith like Peter's. A. T. Robertson wrote: "What is the rock on which Christ will build his vast temple? . . . It is the same kind of faith that Peter has just confessed." [1]

[1] *Word Pictures in the New Testament* (Nashville: Broadman Press, 1930), I, 132.

The foregoing assertions are, of course, true. However, there is a sense in which the church was to be built on Peter and the other apostles as the first "living stones" to be laid on the chief cornerstone. Ephesians 2:19–20 states: "Ye are . . . built upon the foundation of the apostles and prophets, Jesus Christ himself being the chief corner stone."

(1) *People of the church.*—Peter was the first to put so clearly into words the confession that Jesus is the Christ, which confession is basic to church membership. "Whosoever believeth that Jesus is the Christ is born of God" (1 John 5:1). All who accept Jesus Christ as Saviour and Lord are "living stones" with which the Master builds. "Ye also, as lively [living] stones, are built up a spiritual house" (1 Peter 2:5).

(2) *Perpetuity of the church.*—Jesus gave assurance that his church, in every age, could experience victory in her attacks on the "gates," the very strongholds, of evil. When he said, "The gates of hell [Greek, *hades*] shall not prevail against it," he was looking forward to the ultimate triumph of the church. Just as the gates of hades (death) could not keep the spirit and body of Jesus in separation, so the gates of hades, or death, will not forever hold those who die in Christ. This promise assures us of the resurrection of the body. The saints of all the ages, who will be reunited in body and spirit, will be the church in glory, the bride of Christ. The keystone doctrine of the New Testament is the resurrection of Jesus, with its corollary, the resurrection of the just and the unjust in the last days.

3. PURPOSE OF HIS CHURCH (16:19–20)

A. T. Robertson wrote: "Here again we have the figure of a building with keys to open from the outside. . . . The same power here given to Peter belongs to every disciple of Jesus in all the ages." [2]

---

[2] Ibid., p. 135

Peter used the keys of the kingdom while here on earth. He used them when he preached that mighty evangelistic sermon on the day of Pentecost (Acts 2) when three thousand entered the kingdom. He used the keys when he led Cornelius, the Gentile, to put faith in Christ as Saviour (Acts 10). Peter, Paul, and others used the keys of the kingdom when they made the decision at the Jerusalem conference to take the gospel to the Gentile world (Acts 15). Every soul-winner is using those keys when he wins another to Christ. The evangelistic church is using the keys and the missionaries around the world are using the keys to open the doors of the kingdom of heaven. The keys are offered to all who are in the church, for the church is the agency for proclaiming the good news of the kingdom of heaven.

"Whatever you forbid on earth must be what is already forbidden in heaven, and whatever you permit on earth must be what is already permitted in heaven" (Matt. 16:19, Williams).[3] "Binding" and "loosing" were current and well-known terms in the times of Jesus. Binding meant to forbid; loosing meant to allow. The responsibility for binding and loosing was shared by all the apostles (John 20:23). Jesus stated it as a function of the church (Matt. 18:17-18).

Peter, along with other leaders in the growing church would have to make some very important decisions and would face many problems in the matter of binding and loosing. They were promised the sanction and help of heaven in these responsibilities. The same type of responsibility is placed on other followers of Christ, and the same promise is theirs.

IV. REDEMPTIVE PLAN AND COST OF DISCIPLESHIP (16:21-28)

Peter made a perfect grade on one examination, but he made zero on the next lesson. When the Teacher was certain

---

[3] Charles B. Williams, *The New Testament in the Language of the People* (Chicago: Moody Press, 1958). Used by permission.

that the twelve knew that he was the Messiah, he then began to teach about how he would establish his kingdom.

1. *Redemption Through Crucifixion and Resurrection of the King* (16:21)

Jesus began teaching a lesson which was hard to understand, that is, that he was to redeem the members of his kingdom by death and resurrection. He announced that he must go to Jerusalem, the center of the most violent opposition to him. He stated that he must suffer crucifixion as a result of the action of the Sanhedrin, a judicial body composed of chief priests, scribes, and elders of the Jews.

The idea of dying to redeem others and of rising again was the plan of heaven. Before this time Jesus had referred to the resurrection only indirectly, as when he had referred to the sign of Jonah. After Peter's confession, Jesus brought the resurrection into the forefront of his teaching. This truth is fundamental to all New Testament doctrine.

2. *Peter Rebuked by the King* (16:22–23)

Peter, who had been so highly commended, became a stumbling block. Perhaps with a sort of patronizing air, he said the crucifixion should never happen to Jesus. He had not learned his new lesson. His comment deeply grieved the Saviour, for it suggested the easy way to kingship—the same temptation to avoid the cross which Satan brought in the temptation upon the high mountain. It was as if Satan, the adversary, was doing it again, so Jesus called Peter Satan. Jesus knew that without a cross there would be no crown. God had revealed the truth which Peter stated in his great confession, but the devil certainly inspired this piece of advice. Peter's remark, and perhaps his attitude, brought one of Christ's severest rebukes: "Get thee behind me, Satan: thou art an offence unto me."

3. *Discipleship Through Cross-bearing* (16:24–26)

The disciples had to be taught that they too were to bear crosses. "Deny himself, and take up his cross" were strange, stern words from Jesus. Self-denial means more than merely refraining from some things. It means to say no to every selfish desire, to every selfish impulse, to every selfish motive.

To take up one's cross means more than bearing a sickness bravely or suffering a misfortune with fortitude. A cross is something that one can avoid if he desires, but which he voluntarily assumes for Jesus' sake and the glory of God. It means obedience to Christ, but it includes much more. Cross-bearing was no light matter for the twelve. Some of them came to their death actually by crucifixion. All of them suffered violence for being Christians, violence which they could have avoided by compromise.

The disciples had a further lesson to learn about the kingdom spirit: that one will "save" the spiritual values of the higher life only by losing, putting aside, the aim to get ahead in life through selfish motives. The Authorized Version reads "lose his life" (v. 25) and "lose his own soul" (v. 26). The same word, meaning "life," is used in both passages (see Matt. 16:25–26, RSV). The meaning in each case may be interpreted as "lose his soul-life," or the spiritual and eternal values of life.

It is poor profit to gain all the fame, fortune, and fun of the fleshly life, which last for so short a time, and to lose all the unending and eternal treasures of heavenly living. Some temporal things which are lost in life can be brought back, but lost spiritual treasures are lost forever.

The highest choice dictates the life of self-sacrifice and service, which brings the greater gain. The masses are too blind spiritually to see this truth. Many in the kingdom of heaven, however, lose themselves in service for the King and find themselves possessed of his choicest gifts.

4. *Rewards for Cross-bearing and Obedience* (16:27–28)

The blessed hope for those in the kingdom is that the King is going to return to the earth to consummate his kingdom, that he will come in the glory of the Father with his angels, and that he will reward every disciple who has been faithful. This reward is more than just being saved. Salvation is by grace and not by works; rewards are for the saved, given according to their works. A man is saved by what Jesus did for him; he is to be rewarded for what he does for Jesus.

When Jesus said, "There be some standing here, which shall not taste of death, till they see the Son of man coming in his kingdom," he could have been referring to the transfiguration, or to the destruction of Jerusalem in A.D. 70. Various people interpret the passage in various ways, but the underlying truth is the same. All will be rewarded if they have established the reign of Jesus in their hearts and if they have been faithful to him in cross-bearing testimony.

FOR RESEARCH AND DISCUSSION

1. When the parable of the sower is applied to the message of salvation, which of the four soils represent saved people and which represent unsaved people?
2. Name some of the values of the kingdom of heaven which make it like the pearl of great price.
3. Why did the Pharisees want to kill Jesus?
4. Name some crosses modern Christians should voluntarily assume and bear.

CHAPTER 7

7

The King Teaches Spiritual and Social Principles

Matthew 17–20

WHICH event in the life of the Lord on earth would you rather have witnessed? High among his many exalted experiences was the mountain-top transfiguration. This wondrous scene came after Jesus began to teach about his impending death and to turn his face toward Jerusalem. The transfiguration was a transcendent new revelation about the mysteries of the kingdom.

I. GLORIFICATION AT THE CONSUMMATION OF THE KINGDOM (17:1–13)

Jesus had said that there were some of the disciples who would "not taste of death" until they should "see the Son of man coming in his kingdom" (16:28). The transfiguration satisfies the demands of this promise with awe-filled reality.

About a week after making the promise, Jesus took Peter, James, and John up a high mountain, probably one of the lofty spurs of snow-capped Mount Hermon, in the general area of Caesarea Philippi. These three disciples seem to have been the most understanding of the twelve. Jesus was transfigured before them; that is, he took on the form of his glorified nature, in which he will appear at the consummation of the kingdom.

One Gospel writer says Jesus was praying (Luke 9:28–29). When was he so likely to be transfigured as when he was talking to the Father? The heavenly vision shone out like a diamond on black velvet. Jesus' face was as brilliant as the sun; his clothing was brighter in the shadows than the driven snow in the coves of Mount Hermon. His appearance glittered like the stars above; he dazzled the eyes of the apostles. His deity shone through the veil of the flesh. Even so we may expect him to appear when he comes in the glory of the Father with his angels.

Two celestial messengers, Moses and Elijah, came to hold high conversation with Jesus about his death. Moses represented the Law; Elijah represented the Prophets. Their presence revealed that both the Law and the Prophets assented to the establishment of the kingdom of Jesus through sacrifice—a truth exceedingly hard for the disciples to believe.

B. H. Carroll has pointed out that the transfiguration was a vision and picture of the resurrection experience yet to come, when Christ's kingdom will be consummated and he will appear in glory with his bride. Moses represented the dead in Christ who shall appear then in glory; Elijah represented those Christians who will be alive when Jesus comes, who will be changed and glorified.[1] "We shall not all sleep, but we shall all be changed, in a moment, in the twinkling of an eye, at the last trump: for the trumpet shall sound, and the dead shall be raised incorruptible, and we shall be changed" (1 Cor. 15:51–52).

The transfiguration was a supernal revelation of the coming glory in the kingdom of heaven. It was a mighty encouragement to Jesus, who was facing the fearful crucifixion. It was an overpowering incentive to the apostles to render sacrificial service for his glory.

The three apostles could never forget the vision. Many years later John wrote: "We beheld his glory, the glory as of the only begotten of the Father" (John 1:14). Peter wrote:

---

[1] *An Interpretation of the English Bible* (Nashville: Broadman Press, 1942), p. 24.

"This voice which came from heaven we heard, when we were with him in the holy mount" (2 Peter 1:18).

It was just like Peter to make a foolish remark when exhilarated by so exalted an experience. To perpetuate that experience he wanted to build three booths out of tree limbs, such as the Jews made at their Feast of the Tabernacles. But the cloud took Moses and Elijah out of sight. Peter was brought down from his high ecstasy, to be taken to the foot of the mountain, where suffering humanity needed to be served.

A voice came out of heaven, saying, "This is my beloved Son, in whom I am well pleased; hear ye him." The words were God's signature of approval upon Christ's redemptive plan. The admonition meant that Jesus was to supersede Moses and the prophets in commanding the complete allegiance of the apostles and others. Then the gracious touch of the Master's hand and his tender encouragement not to be afraid allayed their fears.

II. Some Principles of the Kingdom (17:14 to 18:14)

Christianity depends upon Jesus himself. Following the account of the transfiguration, Matthew records six instances which reveal how the King embodied the principles of the kingdom in his daily life and teaching. His deity was revealed in the transfiguration; his character was revealed in succeeding events.

1. *Power Through Faith* (17:14–21)

Healing the afflicted boy at the foot of the mountain revealed Jesus' compassion and power in response to faith.

Because of the need of the people, the Saviour refused Peter's suggestion to stay on the lofty mount of transfiguration. It is easy to feel exhilarated when withdrawn from the world of human need. Devotees to the cloister and the monastery seek that kind of escapism. The spirit of the kingdom of heaven expresses itself in the market place or the squalid lane as well as in the place of prayer, in service to needy people as well as in communion with God.

The nine apostles who were left at the foot of the mountain failed in the crisis when the father brought his boy to them to be healed. The enemies of Jesus must have exulted in diabolic glee at the failure of the disciples. Jesus must have felt hurt in his innermost soul. With regal majesty he healed the boy. Thereby he demonstrated the power he had from God through faith.

Possibly Jesus pointed to the transfiguration mountain when he said that faith could remove mountains, even when faith is as small as a mustard seed. A mountain was a well-known Jewish metaphor for difficulty.

2. Conquest Through Sacrifice (17:22–23)

For the third time Jesus revealed that he was to be a suffering servant of Jehovah (cf. 16:21 and 17:12), dying and being raised from the dead for the redemption of men. The disciples could not comprehend the truth that through the way of suffering and death he was to be a living Saviour, to reign forever and ever as King of kings and Lord of lords.

3. Example Through Obedience (17:24–27)

Jesus revealed himself as a King who would perform all duties of a good citizen, whether religious or civic. The tax-gatherers who collected the half-shekel Temple tax commanded by Moses (Ex. 30:11–15) asked Peter if Jesus paid the tax, probably insinuating that Jesus was not a law-abiding citizen. Quickly Peter defended his Lord by saying that he did. However, Peter does not seem to have been sure. Later Jesus met Peter's unspoken question by asking him who paid tribute, conquering kings or conquered nations. When Peter replied that the conquered nations did, Jesus said that likewise he, the Son of God, could claim exemption from paying tax to God's house.

But Jesus was exemplary. He never set a bad example for anyone. He told Peter to catch a fish out of the Sea of Galilee and find a shekel in its mouth, a half shekel for each of them, with which to pay the tax. Matthew does not say that Peter actually did it, but the implication is that he did. Clearly, the incident means that Jesus would deny himself his rightful privileges in order to set a good example before men.

4. *Childlikeness in the Kingdom* (18:1-6)

It is a sad and disgraceful state of affairs when Christians begin bickering with envy and jealousy about who should receive the greatest honor or position or honorary degree or salary. Such bickering is far from Christlike. The twelve began to quarrel about who would be the topmost official in the kingdom of heaven—as we think of the prime minister or secretary of state.

When Jesus was asked who would be the greatest, he took a child as an object lesson. He told his disciples that they were going in the very opposite direction from the kingdom, that they needed to repent, to rethink their way. They were seeking selfishly for promotion above others. Jesus said that a person must have the spirit of a little child or he cannot even get into the kingdom.

Did Jesus mean to say that the twelve were not in the kingdom? (Judas was not.) No, Jesus wanted them to prove that they were in the kingdom by their works, and by having the spirit of childlike humility. The paradox of Christianity is that it teaches humility and at the same time exalts the worth of man.

Jesus understood the impressionable age of childhood, and forcefully warned his followers against becoming a sinful influence upon children. He was not speaking altogether of infants, but of all his children who believe on him. A man who ruins a beautiful life by seducing that one into sin, said Jesus, deserves to have the largest of millstones about his neck and to drown in the deepest place in the sea.

5. Stumbling Blocks in the Kingdom (18:7–11)

Ungodly men often plot with great ingenuity to lead Christians into sin, and then delight in their nefarious success. Apparently such wicked men think the failure of another should ease their own consciences. Woe to such men!

Sometimes the stumbling block comes from one's own self —something as intimate and desirable as one's hand or foot or eye. The amputation of a tempting hand or misguiding foot or evil eye is to be chosen rather than to have all of one's life cast into the Gehenna fire of sin and everlasting torment. Temptations must be shunned, no matter what the cost.

Even Christ's own followers need to be warned against becoming stumbling blocks (v. 10). Jesus seems to have referred to all his believers as his "little ones." He taught that God's angels, his ministering spirits, watch over all who are in the kingdom.

6. Individual Worth in the Kingdom (18:12–14)

Human personality is the most priceless thing in God's creation. No other religion exalts the individual so highly as he is exalted in the kingdom of heaven. To illustrate this truth, Jesus gave the parable of the good shepherd who sought the lost sheep and rejoiced to find it. No individual, even though debauched in sin and degraded in soul, is unimportant in the kingdom of heaven. One difference between the King of the kingdom of heaven and other religious leaders is that Christ reveals God as lovingly seeking men to save them, while leaders in all other religions advocate methods by men to placate their angry gods.

III. INSTRUCTIONS CONCERNING SOCIAL RELATIONSHIPS
   (18:15 to 19:15)

Some have erred in promulgating a so-called "social gospel." Certainly, we repudiate any doctrine which omits the need for individual regeneration. However, let us remember that the kingdom of heaven has to do with our dealings one with another. It reaches into every area of human relationships. Its outreach is both vertical and horizontal—vertical regarding the relationship of men to God, horizontal regarding the relationships between men and men.

1. *Relationships in the Church* (18:15–20)

Ethics find their highest expression in the social relationships of members of a New Testament church. The personal application of the gospel in the church was taught by Jesus, as recorded in Matthew 16:13–20; the social application of the gospel in the church is taught in the current passage. These two passages are the only records of Jesus' mention of the church. The personal and the social are like the two hemispheres of a perfect and well-rounded whole.

All social difficulties between Christians can be settled if they use the plan of Jesus. The man in the kingdom is to take the initiative in trying to settle the unhappy affair, even though he has been wronged. If the personal approach fails, the Christian is to get one or two wise and fair-minded men to go with him to talk in a Christian manner with the offender. If the obstinate man again refuses to hear, the matter is to be taken to the church as the final court of appeals. There the spirit of love and kindness and fraternity should win any Christian. If the obdurate person refuses the church, his attitude is evidence that he probably is not a Christian. "Let him be unto thee as an heathen man and a publican."

Did Jesus mean that such a one should be given up as

hopeless or consigned to perdition? Never! That was not Christ's attitude toward heathen and publicans. A Christian should seek to win that stubborn man to Christ and to the church; after he is won, a reconciliation will be possible.

Heaven will sanction decisions like this made in the church, said Jesus: "Whatsoever ye shall bind [refuse] on earth shall be bound in heaven: and whatsoever ye shall loose [permit] on earth shall be loosed in heaven." When social relationships are established in the church according to the principles of the kingdom, then heaven approves.

Christ is pictured in the Revelation as being in the midst of his churches. Matthew 18:19–20 records his promise to be in the midst of the smallest congregation, even just two or three, if they are agreeing in prayer together. The words are more than a promise; they are the statement of a fact. Since Jesus is there, the prayer will be answered, although the answer will be as God sees best and not always as the petitioner requests.

2. Forgiveness in the Kingdom (18:21–35)

To forgive is the most difficult of all social adjustments for some people. The teaching about reconciliation within the church stuck in Peter's mind, leading him to ask the very practical question: "Lord, how oft shall my brother sin against me, and I forgive him? till seven times?" He thought he was very generous as he answered his own question. Jesus said forgive "seventy times seven," that is, an unlimited number of times.

Jesus illustrated this teaching with a parable about a high court official, called a servant, who owed his king about $10,000,000 (see footnote, ASV), but the debt was canceled by the forgiving king. However, when the man found an inferior servant who owed him the trifling sum of about $17, he threw the poor fellow into jail.

In addition to the principle of unlimited forgiveness, the

parable teaches many lessons about the relationships between citizens in the kingdom of heaven. It encourages
humility about man's forgiving grace toward man; it exem-
plifies right relationships between people in the church. The
parable illustrates the triviality of the sins of man against
man as compared with the greatness of man's sin against
God. Man enjoys the experience of forgiveness on two conditions, namely, repentance and willingness to forgive the
sins of others. A man in the kingdom must have in his heart
a yearning willingness and desire to forgive.

The kingdom of heaven must include a "system of human
relations, progressively realized, in which the will of God is
the formative principle and all the functions of which are
organized and operated for the purpose of helping all men
to realize the spiritual possibilities of humanity." [2]

Jesus taught many social principles of the kingdom while
he journeyed east of the Jordan en route to Jerusalem—
leaving his beloved Galilee, to see it no more until after the
resurrection.

3. Divorce and the Kingdom (19:1–12)

Those determined Pharisees thought they could trap Jesus
by getting him to take sides on the vexing divorce question.
When they asked if a man was justified in putting away his
wife for every cause, they reflected the liberal view of the
popular school of Hillel. That school permitted divorce for
such petty causes as a woman talking to a man in public or
burning the bread for breakfast, or not covering the head,
or being childless.[3]

Perhaps the Pharisees wanted to get Jesus into trouble

---

[2] Charles S. Gardner, *The Ethics of Jesus and Social Progress* (New
York: George H. Doran Co., 1914), pp. 84–85. Used by permission of
Doubleday & Co., Inc. copyright owners.

[3] J. W. Shepard, *The Christ of the Gospels* (Nashville: The Par-
thenon Press, 1939), p. 452.

with Herod Antipas, who had beheaded John the Baptist because of his denunciation of Herod's conduct on this very question. Divorce was one of the most perplexing yet most important social problems of that day, as it is now. The most important social contract is marriage; the most important social institution is the home. Jesus went back to God's original purpose for marriage. He revealed the eternal and binding nature of the marriage vow, as God first intended it. God meant the family to be a miniature picture of the kingdom.

The Pharisees, when foiled by the clear answer of Jesus, next tried to entrap him into contradicting Moses. They asked why Moses permitted divorce (Deut. 24:1). Jesus explained that Moses actually raised the standards regarding divorce by demanding that a man write a legal bill of divorcement. Before Moses' provision, a man could divorce his wife merely by publicly announcing his plan to do so.

The low standard was man's, not God's. Ungodly men have maintained tragically low standards for women and for marriage throughout history—in the time of Moses, with the Jews during the life of Christ, and everywhere in paganism where Jesus has not influenced society.

Jesus outlined specific principles about divorce and remarriage. He taught about the ethics involved rather than their customs. Customs change; principles are invariable, unchangeable, and eternal. Jesus clearly taught that the marriage vow was ordained of God in creation to be indissoluble except by death or adultery.

The sanctity of the marriage vow is the foundation of a Christian social order. Break that up and all Christian society will be overthrown. Marriage is the heart of Christian society; if the heart is sick, the whole body is sick.

The disciples were shocked, as some people are today, by this teaching of Jesus. They thought it terrible to be married indissolubly to the same woman under unfortunate conditions. They suggested that it might be better not to marry.

Jesus said some are born incapable of successful marriage, some are made that way by men, and some deliberately choose not to marry. He himself and John the Baptist did not marry. If some should choose celibacy, believing they could be more successful in promoting the kingdom of heaven if unmarried, they had his sanction. However, he recognized that few are called to follow this course.

4. *Children and the Kingdom* (19:13–15)

There is no place on earth ten miles square where women and children are safe when alone or are respected in society equally with men, unless the influence of Jesus and the kingdom of heaven has made it so.

After telling how Jesus exalted womanhood and family life, Matthew relates one of the tenderest of scenes, when Jesus, lover of children, blessed the little children. He was indignant that the disciples thought children were too insignificant for his loving attention. His saying: "Suffer little children, and forbid them not, to come unto me: for of such is the kingdom of heaven," is the "bill of rights" for childhood.

Jesus used this incident to emphasize again that the spirit of the kingdom of heaven is the childlike spirit. He touched the children with his blessing hands and prayed for them. By this he accomplished two things: he declared that the childlike spirit of faith and love qualified one for the kingdom, and he put a halo of glory upon childhood as being of infinitely great importance in a Christian social order.

IV. SOME QUESTIONS RELATED TO THE KINGDOM (19:16 to 20:34)

1. *Riches and the Kingdom* (19:16–30)

While Jesus was en route to Jerusalem, a rich but hungry-hearted ruler literally ran and knelt before the Master, asking, "Good Master, what good thing shall I do, that I may have eternal life?" He seemed to the world to have everything, but he lacked the best things. He lacked peace with God and joyous fellowship with his fellowmen.

Jesus turned the seeker's attention toward God immediately, for the one good thing in life must come from the only one who is wholly good. The ruler claimed that from his youth he had been obedient to the commandments which relate to men. The Saviour loved him. Then Jesus put his finger on the sensitive spot in his life by telling him to give all his accumulated wealth to the poor.

The disappointed young man went away into oblivion, sadly unable to meet the test of love of money versus loyalty to Christ. Jesus had exposed the fact that the seeker was breaking the spirit of all the commandments and the spirit of the kingdom. He had put gold on the throne of his heart, and he loved self more than he loved his poverty-stricken neighbors. Love of money is one of the gravest and most dangerous of social and spiritual problems.

Jesus did not oppose wealth itself, nor did he demand that all who would be spiritual were to renounce it. He did not advocate the communistic or socialistic theory. He did not outline any formal system of distribution of wealth.

Jesus was concerned about the influence of the spiritual over the economic. He advocated the kingdom principle of subordination of the love of money to the love of God, of stewardship of material wealth as a trust from God. Jesus demanded a positive personal righteousness toward God and a positive social righteousness toward needy, suffering humanity.

"It is easier for a camel to go through the eye of a needle, than for a rich man to enter into the kingdom of God," said Jesus as the rich young man went away sorrowfully. Entrance into the kingdom for a rich man—or any other—is impossible without the help of God above, without a spiritual transformation. The love of money carries with it many temptations to go contrary to the kingdom of heaven. A rich man is tempted to love money devotedly, to hoard it selfishly, to trust it entirely, to worship it supremely, and to use it sinfully. To possess it is not a sin, but it can become a terrific danger to one's soul and destiny.

Talkative Peter spoke again. He asked what they who had left their homes and fishing business to follow Jesus were going to get out of it. He was assured that "in the regeneration"—the coming of a new heaven and a new earth—all who had sacrificed to follow Jesus would have rewards of glory and power in the kingdom of heaven.

Jesus used the illustration of a monarch on his throne with his dignitaries sitting around him on lesser thrones of judgment. However, he denied that there would be any priority rights in the kingdom, for all reward will be according to divine grace. Every one who shares in the labor and sacrifice of the kingdom will share in its power and glory.

2. Laborers and Wages in the Kingdom (20:1-16)

The parable about the householder who employed laborers at different hours of the day illustrates how the first may be last and the last first (19:30). The lesson could apply to the twelve who wanted priority in glory, or to the general subject of entering the kingdom in youth, middle age, or old age. The laborers received the same wages, no matter how long they worked.

Jesus was impressing several truths: that rewards are to be given according to the grace and bounty of the sovereign King; that every laborer will receive his fitting reward; and that every kingdom worker is precious in the sight of God. All can trust the King to do right about rewards. All should work from the motive of love rather than from a desire for reward. Note that those who trusted without bargaining (vv. 4, 7) received more than they expected.

3. *The Cross and the Kingdom* (20:17–19)

For about six months following the transfiguration, the Lord experienced an intensification of the divine compulsion which was driving him toward crucifixion. He felt he should prepare the twelve by showing them how he must suffer and sacrifice to win his kingdom. He gave them some details about his forthcoming condemnation by the Jewish Sanhedrin and the torturous crucifixion by the Romans.

The understanding of the apostles was so blinded by preconceived ideas about how the Messiah should rule that it seems to have been impossible for them to understand or believe that he would be put to death. Jesus knew full well that a Redeemer-King's crown must be linked to a cross.

4. *Greatness in the Kingdom* (20:20–28)

Some of the basic social principles of the kingdom concept had been taught. The redemptive principle had been emphasized. The twelve apostles needed another lesson about the way greatness is attained in the kingdom.

Salome, the wife of Zebedee, and possibly the sister of Mary the mother of Jesus, asked that her sons, James and John, might have the highest rank in the protocol of the kingdom. She asked that they might sit on the chief seats of honor, next to the King. Jesus gently reproved their ambition by asking if the two young men could drink the cup—pay the price—by which he himself was to obtain his throne.

When they confidently declared that they could, the Saviour did not challenge them. Indeed they later proved that they could pay the price, for James went to a martyr's death (Acts 12:2) and John had a baptism of suffering through both imprisonment and exile.

The other apostles reacted with intense resentment against these two (whom some Bible students think were cousins of Jesus) for scheming to get honors by trying to overreach their colleagues. The whole episode reveals how little any of the apostles knew about the nature of the kingdom and how little of its spirit they possessed.

Jesus taught them that true greatness in the kingdom was not to be attained by favoritism or political wire-pulling. They had yet to learn to travel the royal road to greatness through service. The world believes greatness comes by being a monarch with servants, or being a conquerer on a battlefield, or being a man with more wealth than his fellows. Rank is not thus measured in the kingdom of our Lord. The one who serves others most is the greatest.

5. *Compassion of the King* (20:29-34)

Jesus the King demonstrated the spirit of service to needy humanity when he stopped to show compassion toward two lowly and pitiful blind men. He was amid the throngs that crowded around him as he journeyed toward Jerusalem. The blind men cried in persistent and plaintive appeals for him to open their eyes. When he had restored their vision, they followed their great benefactor. The King was always majestic in his compassion, whether he was healing helpless blind men or dying on a cross to save sinners.

FOR RESEARCH AND DISCUSSION

1. Why was it appropriate for Moses and Elijah to appear at the transfiguration? What did they represent?
2. How can one be ambitious to rise in rank and yet be a good citizen of the kingdom?
3. How can a Christian prove that he has forgiven another in his heart?
4. What did Jesus say about remarriage after divorce?
5. How can riches be made a mighty kingdom power in a man's life, rather than a terrific temptation?
6. Name some people in your church or community who measure up high according to the standards of Jesus for greatness.

CHAPTER 8

I. FORMAL CLAIMS OF KINGSHIP (21:1 to 22:14)
   1. The Triumphal Entry (21:1–11)
   2. Cleansing the Temple (21:12–17)
   3. The Rebuke to Unfruitfulness (21:18–22)
   4. The King's Authority Challenged (21:23–32)
   5. Warning to Israel (21:33 to 22:14)

II. EFFORTS TO ENSNARE THE KING (22:15–46)
   1. About Civil Obedience (22:15–22)
   2. About the Resurrection (22:23–33)
   3. About the Law (22:34–40)
   4. Jesus Shows That He Is the Son of God (22:41–46)

III. WOES UPON THOSE WHO REJECT THE KING (23:1–39)
   1. Pharisaism Exposed and Denounced (23:1–12)
   2. Woes Like Thunderbolts (23:13–36)
   3. Lament over Jerusalem (23:37–39)

IV. PROPHECIES RELATED TO THE KINGDOM (24:1–51)
   1. The Destruction of Jerusalem
   2. The Second Coming of Christ
   3. The End of the World

V. INSTRUCTIONS ABOUT THE CONSUMMATION OF THE KINGDOM (25:1–46)
   1. The Importance of Being Ready (25:1–13)
   2. Reward of the Faithful (25:14–30)
   3. The Kingdom Established (25:31–46)

8

The King Claims Kingship and Again Is Rejected

Matthew 21–25

A ROMAN KING or a victorious general who returned after a successful campaign in war was acclaimed by a triumphal procession into the city. The Senate led the parade, followed by trumpeters, flute players, captives, spoils of war, and oxen for sacrifices. Captive kings and their chieftains were chained together and driven along. Then came the conquering hero in his chariot, ostentatiously attired in purple and gold, his scepter in his hand. The ovation was tumultuous; the feasting was riotous; the spirit of carnival was universal.

How different was the triumphal entry of the meek and lowly Jesus! No Roman conqueror ever rode with such majestic kingliness as did the humble Man of Galilee who went into the city of David on a borrowed donkey, amid the hosannas of the multitude. Thus he was formally claiming to be the King of the kingdom of heaven.

I. FORMAL CLAIMS OF KINGSHIP (21:1 to 22:14)

The hour had come for Jesus to reveal himself as the fulfilment of the prophecies about the King of the kingdom. God had promised David: "I will stablish the throne of his kingdom for ever" (2 Sam. 7:13). God had further said: "Ask of me, and I shall give thee the heathen for thine inheritance" (Psalm 2:8). "Of the increase of his government and peace there shall be no end, upon the throne of David, and upon his kingdom" (Isa. 9:7).

Daniel prophecied: "In the days of these kings shall the God of heaven set up a kingdom, which shall never be destroyed" (Dan. 2:44). Zechariah had said: "Rejoice greatly, O daughter of Zion; shout, O daughter of Jerusalem: behold, thy King cometh unto thee: he is just, and having salvation; lowly, and riding upon an ass, and upon a colt the foal of an ass" (Zech. 9:9).

1. The Triumphal Entry (21:1–11)

The thesis of the Gospel of Matthew could not have been dramatized more picturesquely than by the triumphal entry of Jesus into Jerusalem in fulfilment of the prophecy of Zechariah. Jesus initiated the demonstration purposefully, generating widespread and excited enthusiasm. He could not have chosen a more dramatic time than the Passover, when multitudes crowded Jerusalem on that celebrated feast day. He left Bethany and came to Bethphage, where he procured an ass with her colt. He was received in the city and acclaimed like a king, with hosannas shouted and palm branches and garments spread in the road before him.

Earthly kings rode with their steeds gaudily draped; he sat upon the garments of his admirers. Earthly kings were praised by soldiers and noblemen; he was acclaimed by children and peasants. Earthly kings were received by show of swords and spears; he was acclaimed with palm branches and boughs of trees. Earthly kings rode on war horses; Jesus the Prince of peace rode upon the foal of an ass. A heart of love was his panoply, as was becoming to one who came to be sovereign over the hearts of the people. Jesus accepted their acclaim: "Hosanna to the Son of David: Blessed is he that cometh in the name of the Lord." It was appropriate to his kingly role. The whole city was excited. The exultant cry implied the messiahship of Jesus, and that his acceptance of their praise without protest was equal to an affirmation of the claim. Jesus silenced his enemies by claiming a fulfilment of Psalm 8:2: "Out of the mouth of babes and suck-lings hast thou ordained strength" (cf. Matt. 21:16).

2. *Cleansing the Temple* (21:12–17)

The die was cast! The day after Jesus had claimed his kingship by means of his triumphal entry (Mark 11:12–19), he went into the part of the Temple called the court of the Gentiles. Multitudes of faithful Jews were there from afar with no sacrifices but what they could buy on the spot. Some of the local Jews were alert to make a pretty profit, selling animals and doves. Others were changing foreign money into the Temple currency, with which sacred dues must be paid. Naturally, they could receive a handsome rate of ex-change. The court was like a furious bargain day in an Ori-ental bazaar. The worship of God was forgotten; the worship of mammon prevailed. Jesus drove out the greedy, noisy traders.

By cleansing the Temple, Jesus demonstrated his kingship in several ways. He drove the money changers out with the authority of his righteousness and holy zeal. He quoted Isaiah (56:7), who said that the house of God should be a house of prayer. Then he quoted Jeremiah (7:11), charging the religious rulers with making the Temple "a den of thieves." After the avaricious traders were dispelled and their money-changing tables were overturned, Jesus proved his authority by healing the blind and lame people there.

3. *The Rebuke to Unfruitfulness* (21:18–22)

Bringing a curse on the fig tree was not done in a fit of temper because Jesus was hungry; it evidently was done to teach a lesson about the kingdom of heaven. Figs appear on trees before the leaves. Though it was not the season for figs, this tree had a profusion of leaves but no fruit. To Jesus the leafy, fruitless tree was like the Pharisees and others whose religious formalism had not produced spiritual fruit. "By their fruits ye shall know them." Furthermore, Jesus used this event to teach the place and power of faith and prayer in the kingdom. Whatever a Christian asks under the guidance of the Holy Spirit, believing, he will receive.

4. The King's Authority Challenged (21:23–32)

The popularity and powers of Jesus were more than the Sanhedrin leaders could endure. They asked him a subtle question about his authority for teaching and performing miracles. If he claimed authority from God, they would accuse him of blasphemy. If he claimed authority from men, they would say it should have been from the Sanhedrin. If he claimed royalty, he would have trouble from the Romans.

Wisdom from above enabled Jesus to avoid these difficulties. He answered by asking a question about the authority of the baptism of John: Was it from heaven or from man? His opponents could not risk saying that it was from men, for they feared the multitude, who adored the martyr John as a prophet. They could not say it was from God, because John had proclaimed Jesus as the Messiah. Jesus was thus declaring that his authority was from heaven. The claims of the chief priests and elders to be authorities on religious matters were discredited when they said they did not know the answer to the question of Jesus.

Jesus then told of two sons who were commanded to work in their father's vineyard. One curtly refused, but later repented and went to work. The other boastfully said he would go, contrasting himself favorably with the son who refused, but he did not go.

Jesus showed that the group who sought to oppose him were like this latter boy, boasting their superior goodness but manifesting their disobedience. The despised tax collectors and prostitutes who repented would enter the kingdom before those who professed but did not practice. John the Baptist had preached and baptized according to the way of righteousness, and these chief priests and scribes had heard, but they had not repented.

5. *Warning to Israel* (21:33 to 22:14)

After Jesus had exposed the unbelief of the religious leaders toward John the Baptist and himself, he clearly foretold the judgment which would come to those unbelievers and the nation itself.

The meaning of the parable could not be misunderstood. The wicked husbandmen, or sharecroppers, represented the nation of Israel. The servants were the prophets of God who had been slain throughout Israel's history. The son whom the sharecroppers slew was the Son of God, whom they would soon crucify. The return of the absentee landowner and his wrath represented the judgment of God to come on Israel.

In his metaphor about the stone that was rejected and yet became "the head of the corner," Jesus forcefully predicted that the gospel of the kingdom would be preached to the Gentiles and accepted by them. Perverse, insistent rejection of Christ would result in judgment (v. 41). Making clear that he himself would become "the head of the corner," Jesus continued: "This is the Lord's doing, and it is marvellous in our eyes" (cf. Psalm 118:22–23).

Jesus became more specific. In the parable about the marriage feast of a king's son, he was asserting his kingship. The Jews expected the kingly reign of the Messiah to be ushered in with a feast, at which they believed that only Jews would be present. In the parable, the first people invited to the feast represented the Jews. The messengers who were killed represented their prophets. The bad and the good people who were invited in from the highways— like modern hitchhikers and hoboes—meant the Gentiles.

The main point of emphasis was that the armies were sent to destroy those murderers and to burn their cities. Were the words of Jesus meant to foreshadow the judgment of God on Israel, when Jerusalem would be destroyed and the nation scattered? Perhaps such a meaning was included. However, the individual application is also included.

Gentiles and Jews alike must wear the garments of holiness and righteousness if they participate in the blessings of the kingdom. Those without the righteousness which the King requires (and provides) may expect the horrors, the weeping, and the torments of the place prepared for all who choose to remain outside the kingdom of blessedness. "Many are called, but few are chosen." God calls, but only those who answer the call are chosen for blessedness. God's sovereignty and human responsibility go hand in hand.

II. EFFORTS TO ENSNARE THE KING (22:15–46)

Various groups of men with conflicting beliefs combined for a direct attack on Jesus. They hoped to entangle him in trouble with the Roman government or to discredit him with the people who hailed him as king.

1. About Civil Obedience (22:15–22)

Mutual opposition to an enemy can make strange bedfellows. Even Pharisees and Herodians united in an effort to ensnare Jesus. They began with flattering talk but concluded with a dangerous question about whether to pay tax to Caesar or not. If Jesus had said pay it, a storm of protest would have risen from the Pharisees. If he had said not to pay it, the Herodians would have seen that he was arraigned before the Romans for civil disobedience.

Jesus asked for a coin. It had Caesar's image on it. He said, "Render therefore unto Caesar the things which are Caesar's; and unto God the things that are God's." In indicating life's dual responsibilities, our Lord also furnished the principle upon which Baptists and others have enunciated the doctrine of the separation of church and state. Jesus refused to become a revolutionary rebel against Rome; he taught men not to become revolutionary rebels against God.

2. About the Resurrection (22:23–33)

When certain of the Sadducees, the most powerful sect in Jerusalem, saw Jesus overcome the Pharisees and Herodians, they propounded a question about the future life—in which they did not believe. They brought up a question involving a practice sanctioned by Moses (Deut. 25:5) whereby a man should marry his brother's widow. They stated a hypothetical case, where one woman married seven brothers successively. "Whose wife shall she be of the seven?" was their cynical query.

This group of Sadduces were trying to lead Jesus either to deny Moses or to offend the Pharisees, who believed in the resurrection. Again Jesus cut through to the heart of the question, saying that the God of Abraham was not the God of the dead but of the living. Belief in the resurrection was vital to Jesus because his resurrection was to be the doctrinal keystone of the Christian faith.

It is said that a great man of science, Michael Faraday, once heard a student sneer at the mention of the resurrection of the body. As the story goes, Faraday threw a silver goblet into a jar of acid, which completely dissolved it. Then he threw in a substance which precipitated the silver on the bottom of the jar. He later took the silver to a silversmith who made it into a goblet more beautiful than before. The teacher then said: "If I, an ordinary scientist, can dissolve and remake a silver goblet, is it a thing incredible that God can raise the body from the dead?"

3. About the Law (22:34–40)

The Pharisees, apparently elated that Jesus had silenced the Sadducees, again tried to trap him. A scribe, that is, a copyist and interpreter of the law of Moses, asked what type of commandment was the weightiest and most important.

Jesus, with his marvelously incisive mind, summed up in the all-inclusive word "love" all the duties of true religion and all social obligations. Love for God sums up the first four of the Ten Commandments; love for men sums up the last six. Love for God is the personal side of true religion; love for men includes the social relationships.

4. *Jesus Shows That He Is the Son of God* (22:41–46)

After Jesus had silenced all his critics, he counterquestioned them regarding the person of the messianic King: "What think ye of Christ? whose son is he?" It was a question about the essential nature of the kingdom of heaven. They said the Messiah was the son of David. Jesus quoted from Psalm 110:1, a messianic psalm, saying, "If David then called him Lord, how is he his son?" The Messiah was David's Lord. Thus, Christ definitely answered the challenge to his authority by showing that he had the authority of Deity as well as humanity. As defeated people often do, his enemies resolved to retaliate by violence.

III. WOES UPON THOSE WHO REJECT THE KING (23:1–39)

The righteous indignation of Jesus exploded. He laid bare the hypocrisy of his opponents. They were eyeservants and men-pleasers; they practiced external showmanship of holiness in creed and conduct; they sought pre-eminence and position. They were loud in their professions of piety.

1. *Pharisaism Exposed and Denounced* (23:1–12)

Jesus said the scribes of the Pharisees sat "in Moses' seat," that is, they held the position of authoritative teachers. Jesus commended the teachings of Moses, but he unrelentingly criticised the conduct of these teachers. They mercilessly loaded the people with hundreds of laws about religious ceremony, all of which came from their man-made traditions.

Again, Jesus accused them of ostentatious showmanship of their religion. The command of Moses about keeping the law close to them and in their minds (see, for example, Deut. 6:8; 22:12) had become a mere outward ritual. During the interbiblical period, the Pharisees began to enclose certain passages of the Law in small leather containers called phylacteries, and to bind them to their foreheads. Through the years various leaders had made these phylacteries larger and larger, in order to demonstrate unusual piety. This outward display was in strict contrast with the spirit of Jesus, who said, "Do not your righteousness before men, to be seen of them" (6:1, ASV).

Another accusation was about social ambition, pride in sitting near the hosts at banquets, delight in being fawned on by men in public. Another charge was that they loved authority over others, loved to be called Rabbi—not unlike the anxiety of some now to be called Doctor.

2. Woes Like Thunderbolts (23:13–36)

Woes inevitably come to men and nations who reject Jesus, who break the laws of the kingdom of heaven, who live in hypocrisy and practice unrighteousness. When Jesus said, "Woe," it may have meant, "Alas to you," expressing his sorrow mingled with his wrath. Plummer says: "These seven Woes are like thunder in their unanswerable severity, and like lightning in their unsparing exposure." [1]

The first woe (v. 13) was hurled against the scribes and Pharisees for marching up to the gates of heaven but not entering nor allowing others to enter. They had heard John the Baptist identify Jesus as the Messiah. Jesus had been

---

[1] Alfred Plummer, *An Exegetical Commentary on the Gospel According to St. Matthew* (Grand Rapids: Wm. B. Eerdmans Publishing Co., 1910), p. 316.

teaching and preaching the kingdom since that time; yet these Pharisees refused to enter, and they influenced others not to believe on Christ. (Some manuscripts include another woe here.)

In the second woe (v. 15) Jesus charged that the Pharisees were overzealous to proselyte others into their own sect, who in turn were more fanatical about the outward pretense of religion than the Pharisees themselves. They became twice as bad as their teachers and were worthy to be called the sons of Gehenna, the place of torment.

The third woe (v. 16) accused the Pharisees of being blind guides, leading others into dishonesty and untruth. They said if they swore by one thing the oath was binding; if they swore by another it was not binding, and they were not compelled to carry it out. They had developed a notorious system of rationalized lying. It was as puerile as when children cross their fingers while telling a lie, saying it does not count. Jesus abhorred their falsity. In the kingdom of heaven a Christian's statement should not need an oath.

Pharisaism was built on strict obedience to hundreds of rules about ethics and ceremony (see v. 23). The Pharisees were scrupulous in their concern to tithe even the little garden herbs, while they ignored such all-important matters of righteousness as justice, mercy, and faith. Jesus did not blame them for their honesty in tithing; in fact, he said they should do it. He blamed them for their gross lack of a sense of spiritual values. The crowd undoubtedly saw the humor in the hyperbole about straining out a gnat from the wine through a cloth before drinking, and yet swallowing a camel, hump and hoofs and all!

The fifth woe (v. 25) was aimed at their meticulous system of ceremonial cleansing. Their rules were pure tradition, not drawn from Moses' law nor from the prophetic writings, nor did they refer to cleanliness for the sake of health.

Christ, in his sixth woe, (v. 27) compared their outward show of righteousness to the whitewashed burial places commonly seen in Palestine. The tombs looked attractive on the outside but were foul with decay on the inside. Jesus said the hearts of the hypocrites were like the tombs, full of moral decay and wickedness.

The last woe (v. 29) was concerning the secret and unholy purpose of certain of the Pharisees who were determined to kill Jesus. The Jews professed great humiliation that their wicked ancestors had slain some prophets of God, so they built elaborate tombs for them. Yet their leaders were plotting to kill one greater than the prophets. He must needs classify them as a brood of snakes, unable to escape the judgment of Gehenna. Upon them would come the blood of all the martyrs, from Abel, who was the first to be murdered, to Zacharias, who was the last martyr to be mentioned in the Jewish Scriptures.

To our own age would not the Master repeat similar "woes"? Perhaps he would say: Woe to you who, while professing to be Christian, permit your attitude and life to become barriers to others who need to know the Lord. Woe to you who are more eager to persuade men to your pet doctrinal interpretation that you are to win them to Christ. Woe to you who will manipulate the facts to your own advantage. In short, woe to you who practice the forms of worship but fail to exemplify its spirit.

3. Lament over Jerusalem (23:37–39)

The Saviour's pointed denunciation of the hypocrisy and wickedness of the Pharisees was followed by an agonizing lament of unrequited love. He had loved and taught and yearned over the beloved city, seeking to prevent disaster, even as a hen protects her brood. But the leaders had rejected the Messiah King, for whom they professed to be waiting. Jesus was brokenhearted. He knew the nation would suffer the consequences. "Your house is left unto you desolate."

The dire calamities which Jesus predicted came within a generation. Titus of Rome came in A.D. 70 and, with cruel reality, fulfilled the prediction. Jerusalem was captured; the Temple was destroyed; the city was razed; multiplied hundreds of the people were crucified; and Israel was scattered to the ends of the Roman world.

Jesus never again taught in the Temple nor on the streets of Jerusalem. He never again offered himself publicly as their messianic King. However, he sounded a note of hope by saying, "Ye shall not see me henceforth, till ye shall say, Blessed is he that cometh in the name of the Lord." He first came in humility; he will return in glory. He came as a servant; he will return as a King. He came as a Saviour; he will return as a Judge. He came to be crowned with thorns; he will return to be crowned with the royal diadem. He came to be crucified; he will return to be glorified.

IV. PROPHECIES RELATED TO THE KINGDOM (24:1–51)

After pronouncing the woes, Jesus left the Temple. The air was electric. Perhaps the disciples wanted to change the subject to relieve the tension. They remarked on the grandeur of the Temple. Such grandeur must have been quite remarkable to these men of Galilee. Immense stones, marble walls, lavish gold plate shining in the sun—all were amazingly beautiful. Jesus predicted that this Temple would be destroyed within the lifetime of some who were living then.

When they sat down on the mountainside east of Jerusalem, the stunned disciples asked: "When shall these things be? and what shall be the sign of thy coming, and of the end of the world?" (v. 3). They associated the Messiah's return with the consummation of the social age in which they were living.

The answer to their questions constitutes what some have called "the sermon on the Mount of Olives." Jesus described the destruction of Jerusalem as a local event, while his second coming was to be universal. The first was to be in their generation; the other was to be in the unforeseeable future. The two events resemble each other in some respects. Christ's descriptions of them are so entwined that it is impossible to be dogmatic about which sentence refers to one and which to the other. His exhortation is clear, that everybody should be watchfully waiting and be ready.

1. The Destruction of Jerusalem

Jesus knew the laws of survival of nations and the symptoms of internal decay. He knew the people of Israel were morally disintegrating. The fanatical attitude of the Jews toward Rome and the attitude of powerful Rome toward rebellious territories made a clash inevitable. The Romans were getting discouraged about making peaceful and loyal subjects out of the Jews. Clearly, certain of the things Jesus said referred to the destruction of Jerusalem. The city was to be utterly devastated (vv. 1–2). His followers would be persecuted and hated because of Christ (vv. 9–10). The "abomination of desolation" prophesied by Daniel would come (vv. 15–21), in which there would be danger, hasty flight, and untold suffering. Jesus said they should pray that it not come on the sabbath, when they were forbidden to journey, nor in winter, when suffering would be intense.

In A.D. 70 Titus of Rome laid seige to Jerusalem and devastated it. The Jewish historian, Josephus, described the suffering and death by famine and slaughter as being inhuman and appalling. The Judaistic religion and way of life were abolished in Palestine; the sacrificial system was abandoned with the destruction of the Temple, and has never been re-established. The people of Israel were scattered to the uttermost parts of the known world.

2. *The Second Coming of Christ*

Possibly some of the predictions in chapter 24 refer both to the destruction of Jerusalem and the return of Christ to the earth. No verse in the chapter can be a dividing point between the two topics. However, as the chapter progresses, the first theme fades and the second is brought into focus.

Believers are warned not to be deceived by false prophets and men who claim to be the Messiah, by wars and rumors of wars, by famines and earthquakes—as some men have been deceived by every world upheaval since then. Patience and endurance through all this were urged in order to attain God's power to inner peace and control of one's soul.

Great world-shaking events are predicted. Christ will come suddenly, unexpected by most people. They will be following the ordinary pursuits of life, as they were when the Flood came. They will be divided, believer from unbeliever, husband from wife, friend from friend. All are urged to be faithful always, and be ready.

The verses beginning with 30 generally tell of the return of Christ, of how he will be crowned king, and of how he will separate his loyal kingdom subjects from the rebellious and unbelieving. Jesus was not encouraging a meticulous study of history and the Scriptures to determine a time schedule showing exactly when to expect him to return: "Of that day and hour knoweth no man." He was teaching about separation of the saved from the lost and the rewards to the righteous faithful.

3. *The End of the World*

"The end of the world" (v. 3) means "the consummation of the age" (see RSV). The Jews thought of "this age" as being wholly evil and "the coming age" under the messianic King as being wholly good.

V. Instructions About the Consummation of the Kingdom (25:1–46)

The Master Teacher had foretold the completion of his kingdom, giving many details. He illustrated these truths with thrilling, human-interest stories.

1. *The Importance of Being Ready* (25:1–13)

No illustration could have caught the attention of the hearers more quickly than one about a marriage. All the world loves a lover. Jesus pictured a typical scene of some maidens waiting for a bridegroom to take his bride to his home. Five prudent girls took sufficient oil for their lamps; five went thoughtlessly unprepared for the long wait. When the lamps of the foolish girls were going out, the wise ones were unable to provide oil for them. The girls who were prepared went in to the wedding feast; the five unprepared ones were kept in outer darkness. This parable emphasizes the joyous salvation of those who are wise enough to prepare and the condemnation awaiting those who are not ready when Jesus comes. Readiness involves application to our Christian duty.

2. *Reward of the Faithful* (25:14–30)

As further inducement to faithfulness in anticipation of his return, Jesus told the parable of a landlord who was going abroad. One servant received five talents (approximately $5,000), one received two talents ($2,000), and one received one talent ($1,000) with which to transact business until the landlord should return. The talents were unequally distributed, just as abilities and opportunities for service are unequal among men. The basis of rewards was not ability nor opportunity nor success, but faithfulness. The man who gained two talents was equally as faithful as he who gained five; so he received the same praise from the landlord.

Jesus was illustrating the place of good works in the Christian life, not explaining how to become a Christian. One is saved by Christ through faith; he will be rewarded by Christ for faithfulness. Salvation is received by grace; rewards are attained by works. The humble Christian who is just as faithful in the use of his possibilities in prayer, Bible study, tithing, and soul-winning as is some notable preacher with greater opportunities will be rewarded equally with the more gifted man. Every Christian can do at least two things which will win rewards when Jesus comes: build a more Christlike character and witness to others in soul-winning.

3. *The Kingdom Established* (25:31–46)

When the Germans overran Belgium in World War I, the king of the Belgians was exiled. After the Allies conquered, the king went back to repossess his kingdom. He reorganized his government, rewarding the faithful with places of honor and usefulness. He then brought all traitors to judgment and punishment according to each man's guilt. Jesus closed the solemn and beautiful "sermon on the Mount of Olives" by picturing a similar scene.

The returning King of the kingdom of heaven will sit on the throne of his glory with his angels about him. He will gather together all people of all time and there separate the believers from the unbelievers. He will reward the righteous, every man according to his responsibility and deeds; he will punish the wicked.

The phrase "inherit the kingdom" is a key term in this passage. To inherit the kingdom involves more than entering the kingdom. Those who have entered the kingdom through faith look forward "to an inheritance . . . reserved in heaven" for them (1 Peter 1:4). Kingdom citizens are joint heirs with the Lord Jesus Christ. Those who are saved have entered the kingdom. However, they will inherit its full riches to the degree in which they have done good works, such as feeding Christ's hungry children, giving water to the thirsty in Christ's name, clothing the naked, and visiting the sick or imprisoned for Christ's sake. One cannot maintain right relations with Christ and ignore his brethren who are hungry, naked, persecuted, and sick. The Scriptures say that the faithful shall sit with him on thrones of glory and reign with him (Matt. 19:28; Rev. 3:21; 20:4). They will inherit the kingdom.

To the unbelieving lost on his left hand, who have not done these deeds of love, the Judge will say: "Depart from me, ye cursed, into everlasting fire, prepared for the devil and his angels." These terrific words from the merciful and loving Christ should settle forever any doubt about the reality of hell. Practically all that is known about hell came from the lips of the gentle Saviour. Hell will not be the same for any two lost persons. Each one will be judged according to his works, his opportunities, and his responsibilities. The kingdom of heaven was prepared for men; the eternal fire of hell was prepared for the devil and his angels. The loving Judge and King of the kingdom does not will that any should perish; men make their own choices as to where they shall go, according to their choices of which master they would serve.

FOR RESEARCH AND DISCUSSION

1. What had been accomplished before the triumphal entry which led Jesus to come out publicly claiming the messiahship?
2. Why is the doctrine of the resurrection important to Christianity?
3. Mention points indicating that Jesus had the brightest mind in all history. From whence came his wisdom?
4. What is the essence of real hypocrisy in religion?
5. In what sense may a believer fail to receive his full "inheritance"?

CHAPTER 9

I. The King Preparing to Suffer Death (26:1–46)
   1. Jesus Prepares His Disciples (26:1–2)
   2. Enemies Prepare for His Murder (26:3–5)
   3. Mary Prepares Jesus for His Burial (26:6–13)
   4. Judas Prepares to Betray Him (26:14–16)
   5. The Disciples Prepare the Passover (26:17–25)
   6. Jesus Prepares a Perpetual Memorial (26:26–30)
   7. He Further Prepares His Disciples (26:31–35)
   8. Jesus Prepares Himself Spiritually (26:36–46)

II. The King Betrayed and Arrested (26:47–56)
   1. Betrayed by a Kiss (26:47–50)
   2. Refuses to Sanction Violence (26:51–54)
   3. Surrenders to the Mob (26:55–56)

III. The King Tried and Crucified (26:57 to 27:66)
   1. Before the Jewish Sanhedrin (26:57–68)
   2. Denied by Peter (26:69–75)
   3. The Betrayer Commits Suicide (27:1–10)
   4. Before Pilate, the Roman (27:11–26)
   5. Crucified, Dead, and Buried (27:27–66)

IV. The King Raised in Triumph (28:1–15)

V. The King Commissions His Disciples (28:16–20)

9

The King Suffers a Cross
to Win a Crown

Matthew 26–28

THE DIVINE tragedy was coming to its climax. The majestic Christ deliberately walked into the valley of the shadow of death, but there was a heavenly light in his soul. He was treading the path to ultimate victory.

I. THE KING PREPARING TO SUFFER DEATH (26:1–46)

It was two days until the Passover feast. (By Jewish counting, Tuesday night was the beginning of Wednesday.) The Sanhedrin was plotting Jesus' death. The darkness of hell was flooding the heart of Judas Iscariot.

1. *Jesus Prepares His Disciples* (26:1–2)

Tuesday night and the next two days were given to intensive preparation for the ordeal ahead. Jesus made the blunt statement that after two days the Son of man would be betrayed to be crucified. His disciples were unable to comprehend so drastic a providence.

2. *Enemies Prepare for His Murder* (26:3–5)

Caiaphas, the high priest, was anxious not to create a riot and incur the wrath of the Romans, for fear they might depose him from the high priesthood. The Sanhedrin gathered together informally in the court of Caiaphas and definitely decided to kill Jesus, but they planned to wait until after the Passover crowds had gone. The amazing offer of

Judas to betray his Lord seemed to the plotting Jews too good to be true.

3. Mary Prepares Jesus for His Burial (26:6–13)

Jesus seems to have spent no night in Jerusalem during the week of the crucifixion, but to have resorted to the little village of Bethany on the slopes of the Mount of Olives.

Tuesday night (Jewish Wednesday) he was at a meal in the home of Simon the leper—presumably someone whom Jesus had cured of leprosy. His beloved friends, Mary and Martha and Lazarus, were there (John 12:2–3). Here was a sweet atmosphere of spiritual fellowship, after the hypocrisy and treachery which Jesus had met in Jerusalem.

The memory of how Jesus raised Lazarus from the dead was vividly fresh in Mary's mind. She took an alabaster flask of very costly ointment called spikenard, broke the cruse, and poured the perfume lavishly on her Master's head. Mary's perfume was worth about a year's wages for a laborer. One cannot love lavishly, as Mary did, without wanting to give lavishly.

The evilhearted Judas became highly indignant that Mary poured out so costly a gift. The generosity of unrestrained love seemed foolish to his selfish heart. Jesus came swiftly to Mary's defense, showing his heartfelt approval of love so extravagant and so generous. He said she had done it to prepare him for his burial.

4. Judas Prepares to Betray Him (26:14–16)

Judas carried the moneybag for the disciples. His dark spirit shown toward Mary revealed his wrong attitude toward money. After being rebuked by Jesus, Judas went to the Sanhedrin and agreed to betray his Lord for thirty pieces of silver (Zech. 11:12). He had already sold himself to the devil. "What will ye give me?" was his motivating question.

5. *The Disciples Prepare the Passover* (26:17–25)

Jesus seems to have rested in Bethany from Tuesday night until Thursday. As a faithful Jewish citizen, he sent the disciples into the city to prepare the Passover feast, commemorating the time when Israel passed out of Egyptian slavery. A comparison of the various accounts by the Gospel writers makes it evident that there were two distinct suppers, the traditional Passover meal followed by the Memorial Supper which Jesus instituted.

At the Passover table Jesus announced that Judas would betray him. One visualizes the well-known masterpiece of Leonardo da Vinci portraying the Passover scene. In it Judas is unmistakable, clutching the moneybag and revealing by the dark features of his face the fear that his design was known. The Saviour is pictured as being heavyhearted but nobly poised, compassionate but sad, regretful but forgiving.

When the wicked Judas asked, "Is it I?" Jesus sadly said it was. It would have been better for such a traitor never to have been born. Alas! the jingle of money was sweeter to him than the bells of heaven. Judas went out, and "it was night" (John 13:30).

6. *Jesus Prepares a Perpetual Memorial* (26:26–30)

Apparently Judas went out before the institution of the Lord's Supper (see John 13:21–30). After Judas left, the atmosphere was more relaxed and the spiritual fellowship more heavenly. Jesus proceeded to establish a beautiful memorial by which some things were to be kept in mind forever. His saved people must always remember his crucified body and shed blood. He perpetuated this memory through sacred drama.

Jesus took bread and blessed it and said, "Take, eat; this

is my body." Here was a lovely piece of Oriental symbolism, a metaphor, like the one when he said, "I am the door," or "I am the vine."

No sacrament with saving grace was intimated; no translation of the bread into the literal flesh of Christ was implied; no glorified body of Christ was miraculously united with the bread; no special blessing of sustaining grace was necessarily imparted; Jesus' action was purely a symbol, a memento, a picture, a memorial. This picture or symbol was given to kindle deep devotion and spiritual affection within the hearts of those who actually meditate upon Christ's sacrificial death. No directive was given about how often it should be observed. Jesus said, "This do in remembrance of me" (Luke 22:19). His word is sufficient.

Likewise, Jesus took a cup of the fruit of the vine, gave thanks, and said, "Drink ye all of it; for this is my blood of the covenant, which is poured out for many unto remission of sins" (Matt. 26:27-28, ASV). It is quite unthinkable that the contents of the cup turned into literal blood. The key word is "covenant" or "testament," a word which the disciples understood.

The blood of the sacrifices on Jewish altars was a symbol of the binding nature of the covenant relationship between God and man, as revealed by Moses. Jeremiah (31:31) had promised a new covenant or contract from God. Jesus said his blood was the seal, or binding symbol, of that new covenant. This fact is to be remembered reverently when one partakes of the Lord's Supper.

The Lord's Supper is retrospective, looking back upon the sacrifice of Jesus for the sins of the world; it is introspective, causing one to search his own soul to see that he partakes of it for a worthy purpose; it is prospective, as it points one's thoughts to the return of the Lord to earth in kingly glory.

Jesus did not face the cross as a defeat. It was a necessary milestone on the way to the throne and crown of the kingdom of heaven. He promised his disciples that they would share in that glory and that they would drink together anew in his Father's kingdom. When the supper was finished, they sang a hymn—some think Psalm 136. This is the only time it is recorded that Jesus sang—when he was under the shadow of the cross. He could sing because the crown was in view.

7. *He Further Prepares His Disciples* (26:31-35)

Unswerving loyalty in the face of sudden crisis and certain danger is difficult. Jesus knew the frailty of human nature. He quoted Zechariah 13:7 to predict that his disciples would be dispersed like sheep when their shepherd is smitten.

One of Peter's besetting sins was self-confidence. He boasted that he could not be made to stumble, no, not he! Christ assured him that before the cock would crow twice—before dawn—Peter would deny him three times. Peter thought he would rather die than deny his Master. The other disciples chimed in with the same boast. When one is strong only in his self-confidence, then he is at his weakest. The prediction of Jesus was sadly and tragically fulfilled.

8. *Jesus Prepares Himself Spiritually* (26:36-46)

Jesus went to his knees in the garden of Gethsemane to prepare himself for the cross. Everyone should go to his knees to prepare to study this experience.

The traditional garden of Gethsemane is on the Jerusalem side of the Mount of Olives, a garden filled with very old and gnarled olive trees. Jesus went with his disciples to this quiet retreat to prepare himself for the fearful morrow. He left eight disciples at the gate, took three deeper into the shadows, and then went forward alone to pray.

Three times Jesus prayed for the cup of death to pass, if

it could be God's will. It was human for him to shrink from death, especially by crucifixion; it was divine for him to say, "Not my will, but thine, be done" (Luke 22:42). Three times the drowsy disciples slept while the agonizing burden of the sins of the world was crushing their Lord. When human sympathy failed, Jesus turned to his heavenly Father.

Satan, the rival contender for world dominion, once more tempted Christ to evade the cross. The salvation of all men hung in the balance. No words can describe the intensity of Christ's prayer; no heart can imagine the agony of his suffering. No human knows all that was involved in the burden that was on his sensitive soul.

When Jesus heard the footsteps of the traitor and the hostile multitude coming to arrest him, he told the disciples to sleep on if they would; their opportunity to share in his prayer burden had passed. A heavily armed mob came, composed of a delegation from the Sanhedrin, some Roman soldiers, and a motley group of others. Jesus had been strengthened from heaven; he went forth majestically to face his foes.

II. THE KING BETRAYED AND ARRESTED (26:47-56)

In all the annals of human history has there ever been a darker day of infamy, a more desperate deed of treachery, and a more shameless act of depravity than when Judas betrayed Jesus into the hands of the Sanhedrin?

1. *Betrayed by a Kiss* (26:47-50)

Few things have revealed the true nature of the unregenerate heart as has the betrayal by a kiss. Matthew used a Greek word meaning that Judas kissed effusively, fondly, much. Jesus, deeply wounded by the treachery of Judas, gave him a searching rebuke when he said, in effect, "Friend, go ahead and do what you came to do."

2. *Refuses to Sanction Violence* (26:51–54)

One of the Gospel writers named Peter as the one who took a sword and swung it with furious intent, trying to cut off the head of a servant of the high priest (John 18:10). It is easy to imagine how the man ducked his head to the side to dodge the swinging blade, and the sword cut off his ear.

Jesus uttered what is universally true: "They that take the sword shall perish with the sword." He refused to sanction violence as a method of advancing the kingdom of heaven. The kingdom way is meekness and self-control. Jesus had settled it in the garden that he was willing to drink the cup of suffering to its depths. He was not helpless. He said he could commandeer twelve legions of angels (72,000) to defend him. His claim that he was fulfilling the Scriptures about the messianic King must have struck terror to the heart of Judas, for he went back to the high priest in remorse.

3. *Surrenders to the Mob* (26:55–56)

Jesus turned to the mob and pointedly asked why they were coming so heavily armed. In truth they were cowards, fearing an insurrection and consequent trouble with the Romans. The majesty of Jesus stands out brilliantly against the dark background of cowardice by the crowd, the treachery of Judas, and the fear of the disciples. All the disciples fled when the emissaries from the Sanhedrin threatened violence. They were like timid sheep after their Shepherd was attacked by the mob.

III. THE KING TRIED AND CRUCIFIED (26:57 to 27:66)

When the accusers took Jesus to trial, the Sanhedrin found it impossible to make a true charge against him. By combining all four Gospel stories we learn that Jesus was arraigned before court six times, three times before Jewish ecclesiastical courts and three times before the Roman civil courts.

1. *Before the Jewish Sanhedrin* (26:57–68)

There was an informal and illegal meeting at the house of Caiaphas, the high priest. The Sanhedrists were quite perturbed at the self-restraint of Jesus, while their false witnesses contradicted one another. Two witnesses finally agreed on what was an utter distortion of his words when he said that if they destroyed the temple (i.e. his body) he would build it back in three days. He had never suggested that he himself might destroy anything, but they testified that he said he might destroy the Temple of worship.

Jesus kept silent. They would have perverted anything he said, and besides, their false accusations were not worth answering. When Caiaphas put Jesus on oath about being the Christ, the Son of God (v. 63), his time had come to declare boldly that he was. In horror the high priest tore his clothing and said Jesus deserved death for blasphemy (Lev. 24:16).

Calmly Jesus predicted his glory at the right hand of power and his return upon the clouds. No defense was introduced. The organized opposition had what they wanted, namely, something with which to clamor for his death. The atrocity and brutality of their blows and spitting were outrageous.

2. *Denied by Peter* (26:69–75)

Peter's love for Christ led him to follow into the court of Caiaphas; his weakness led him to go into panic and to deny Jesus when he was asked if he were a friend of the accused. Three times he denied knowing Jesus, finally cursing and swearing. The first denial led to more violent denials. One lie often leads to a legion of lies. The crowing of the cock was like a fire alarm to Peter's conscience; the sorrowful look of

Jesus was like a dagger piercing his heart. Peter's repentance was bitter and soul-deep. There is a legend that he never heard a cock crow thereafter without weeping.

3. The Betrayer Commits Suicide (27:1–10)

When Judas saw the Sanhedrists taking Jesus to the Romans to ask for a death sentence, the enormity of his crime dawned on him. The Scriptures say Judas was a thief and a devil. He expected Jesus to set up an earthly kingdom of which he would be the treasurer, but he was disappointed.

Judas tried to return the thirty pieces of silver for which he had bargained to betray Jesus, but his deed could not be undone. The ring of the coins as he threw them on the floor—a sound once so sweet to his ears—must have seemed like echoes from the lower regions. The base traitor went and hanged himself.

The priests and elders decided that a good way to use the money involved in the transaction was to buy a potter's field in which to bury strangers—presumably Gentiles who died in Jerusalem.

4. Before Pilate, the Roman (27:11–26)

Since the Romans reserved the authority to issue a death sentence, the Jewish officials took Jesus to Pilate, the Roman governor. Caiaphas had asked if Jesus claimed to be the Son of God; now Pilate wanted to know if he claimed to be a king. Jesus majestically acknowledged that he was a King. When the time was right, the King of the kingdom of heaven declared himself openly.

Pilate seems to have wanted to grant justice to Jesus, but he wanted even more to avoid a Jewish insurrection such as he had experienced before. He thought of a scheme. It was his policy to pardon some criminal on feast days. He would offer the crowd the choice of pardon for Jesus or for a prominent prisoner named Barabbas, who was a robber, murderer and insurrectionist. Some manuscripts add the name Jesus as a surname for Barabbas. Possibly Pilate asked: "Whom will ye that I release unto you, Jesus who is called Barabbas or Jesus who is called Christ?" The name Barabbas means "son of the fathers"; the name Jesus means "savior." The Jews were confronted with the choice of the kind of savior they wanted —one whose name was associated with the patriotic traditions of their fathers or one anointed of God. The chief priests and elders clamored loudly for the pardon of Barabbas and the crucifixion of Jesus.

Pilate cried out in words that have burned into men's hearts through the centuries: "What shall I do then with Jesus which is called Christ?" He washed his guilty hands to no avail; he could not escape the guilt. The Jews said, "His blood be on us, and on our children."

5. *Crucified, Dead, and Buried* (27:27–66)

At this point the Gospel of Matthew admits the reader into the holy of holies of God's revelation of himself. It behooved the Christ to suffer in order to enter into his glory as Saviour and King. He was the Suffering Servant of Jehovah, the Lamb of God, the promised Messiah and the King of kings. The heavenly crown for him was linked to a cross.

The soldiers held a mock coronation of Jesus, jeering at his claim to be a king. A scarlet robe, a crown of thorns, and a reed for a scepter were their degenerate means of derision. They spat in his lovely face; they smote his blessed head; they mocked him as the king of the Jews. When they put the crushing cross on his shoulder, Jesus was physically unable to bear it, being utterly exhausted from a sleepless night, emotional strain, and cruel scourgings. The soldiers impressed into service a man from Cyrene, probably a Jew, to carry the cross.

There is a place on the border of present-day Jerusalem with crevices in the hillside resembling a skull, and with a nearby tomb hewn out of the rock. It strangely fits the description of Golgotha.

When Jesus was brought to Golgotha they gave him a sort of narcotic drink, which he refused. He would drink the cup of suffering to the dregs. The soldiers who nailed the spikes claimed his garments, gambling for the seamless tunic, which perhaps was a loving gift from friends. Jesus suffered indescribable physical torture and mental agony.

Matthew records that over Jesus' head was the accusation: THIS IS JESUS THE KING OF THE JEWS, which was probably the Hebrew version of the inscription that was put there in three languages. Hearts are heavy on reading of the mockings by the passers-by, the Roman soldiers, the Sanhedrists, and even the robbers being crucified with him. They said, "Himself he cannot save." Indeed he could not, if he would give his life as a ransom for many. He was being wounded for our transgressions, bruised for our iniquities.

The enemies challenged, "Come down from the cross, and we will believe." But would they have believed? Emphatically, no. He was dying to make people believe. He knew that being lifted up was the way to draw all men unto himself. It is self-sacrifice, not coming down in compromise, that wins men.

The very sun hid its face at the shameful deed. The spiritual darkness was attended by a blackness that covered the whole land. In that dark hour the Son of God cried, "My God, my God, why hast thou forsaken me?" The human mind cannot know why or in what way he was forsaken of God while he was doing the will of God so magnificently. Doubtless the experience had some relation to his humanity.

A ravaging thirst was burning his tongue. Kind friends gave him some vinegar in a sponge, putting it up to his lips with a reed. It was too late to help. He cried out loudly, and died.

The sacrifices in the Temple were due to be offered at about that hour, with the priests ready to go into the holy of

holies with the blood. That ritual was fulfilled, finished by
Jesus, the great High Priest. He went once for all into the
presence of God the Father to make atonement, just as
priests went behind the veil (see Heb. 9:11–12).

The beautiful veil in the Temple, behind which only the
priests had been allowed to go once a year, was split wide
open from the heaven side down. The entrance into the
presence of God was forever opened to every individual. A
human priest standing between God and any individual now
is an impertinence. Anyone who will may come boldly to the
throne of grace for salvation, without priestly mediation or
sacrament other than that provided by Jesus.

Some friends were faithful to Jesus in his hour of death.
Devoted women sorrowfully stood by to do what they could.
Joseph of Arimathea put the limp body of Christ in a newly
hewn rock tomb. None can realize the gloom over the hearts
of these faithful followers.

But conscience made cowards of the crucifiers. The chief
priests and Pharisees remembered Christ's prediction that he
would rise from the dead on the third day. They secured a
platoon of Roman soldiers from Pilate to guard the grave
securely. He who sits in the heavens must have laughed at
those puny men. They were trying to defeat God, who was
working out his eternal plan of the ages for the salvation of
men.

IV. THE KING RAISED IN TRIUMPH (28:1–15)

Renan was wrong when he wrote *Finis* at the end of his
account of the crucifixion. The King of the kingdom of
heaven rose triumphantly from the dead. The change of the
black despair of the disciples into heavenly hope was not
based on imagination. The Christian church, growing for
nearly twenty centuries, is not founded on a falsehood. The
presence of the living Christ in the hearts of millions is not
an illusion.

The truth of the resurrection was established by many infallible proofs. Matthew introduced four groups of witnesses: the women, the angels, the guards, and the eleven disciples. The resurrection was like the sun smiting the cloud of utter despair and blazoning upon the sky of human faith the rainbow promise of eternal life.

Devoted women went to see the tomb where their Lord had been laid. There they saw an angel from heaven and learned that he had rolled away the stone from the sepulchre door. The guards had fled. The angel announced the resurrection of Jesus and showed the empty tomb.

The women were transported from abject fear to transcendent joy. As they ran to take the good news to the disciples, behold, Jesus himself appeared. The risen Lord sent word that he would meet the disciples in Galilee. There he would have undisturbed opportunity to convince and commission his followers. He was ready to begin a new era in his kingdom plan.

The chief priests tried to suppress the most stupendous news of the ages by bribing the soldier guards to spread a falsehood about the body of Jesus having been stolen away, but their efforts were in vain.

V. THE KING COMMISSIONS HIS DISCIPLES (28:16–20)

The Gospel of Matthew comes to its climax by describing the King of the kingdom of heaven standing on the victorious pinnacle of his resurrection glory, claiming all authority in heaven and on earth. With regal majesty he commissioned his subjects thus: "Go ye therefore, and make disciples of all the nations" (Matt. 28:19, ASV). He promised to go with his subjects as their King, even to the consummation of the new age he was instituting in the world.

In this majestic commission there is one dominant and controlling imperative. The imperative verb is "make disciples" (ASV). The other verbs—"going," "baptizing," "teaching"—are participles. These participles are important, but they are dependent upon the imperative "make disciples." Soul-winning, evangelism, and worldwide missionary conquest are all encompassed in this divine decree. Its fulfilment should be the imperative endeavor of every citizen of the kingdom of heaven, until "the kingdoms of this world are become the kingdoms of our Lord, and of his Christ" (Rev. 11:15).

FOR RESEARCH AND DISCUSSION

1. What was the essential difference between the repentance of Peter and the remorse of Judas?
2. Do you think the saying of Jesus, "They that take the sword shall perish with the sword," relates to going to war for one's country?
3. How was the ceremony of atonement, as described in Leviticus 16, fulfilled by Jesus on the cross?
4. How is the Great Commission (Matt. 28:18–20) binding on Christians today?
5. What in this study of the Gospel of Matthew has impressed you most? has blessed you most?

Suggestions for the Teacher

WHO WILL LEAD IN THE STUDY OF THIS BOOK

The Gospel of Matthew is topically arranged and logically developed, making it delightfully advantageous for teaching. In the majority of instances the chapter divisions are according to topics. By day-after-day review, alert students can fix in memory the essential message of each of the twenty-eight chapters, thereby giving the main stream of thought about the kingdom of heaven as presented in this Gospel.

The required limitation of the length of this book makes the constant use of the Gospel of Matthew imperative. The King James Version is used, but other translations for comparison will be highly instructive.

Purpose

The purpose of the study should be to help class members gain a panoramic view of the contents of the Gospel of Matthew and to interpret them in the light of Jesus' position as King of the kingdom of heaven. The purpose does not include a detailed study of particular passages.

Procedures

Avoid monotony. Even with all the material to be covered in the seven and one-half clock hours of class time, you can use a variety of methods.

Lecture.—The lecture method with modifications, may be used effectively (but not exclusively) by a skilled teacher. Chapter outlines on the chalkboard or a flip chart and open Bibles in the hands of the learners should accompany and supplement the teacher's lecturing.

Reports.—Selected class members may be assigned certain passages on which to prepare reports for class evaluation and discussion.

Discussion.—The suggestions at the end of each chapter "For Research and Discussion" can stimulate some vital class discussion.

Role playing.—In this procedure, a learner puts himself in the place of a certain character, seeking to think and speak as that character would have done in a specific situation.

141

Role playing can contribute to the learner's sympathetic understanding of the position in which the Pharisees and other leaders found themselves. Let one or more class members take the role of Pharisees of Jesus' day and show why they were so loyal to their inherited traditions. The role players should use the Old Testament Scriptures and the history of the nation in the period "between the testaments" to justify their position as Pharisees. The activity should help all the class members to realize how easily we today can slip into a position similar to that of these religious leaders, if we seek to cling to some time-honored custom that may have lost its value and may even be in opposition to the spirit of the New Testament.

Oral reading.—Class time may be used for actual reading from versions other than the King James in an effort to gain exact meanings. Learners should be encouraged to comment on the author's interpretation.

Considering different interpretations.—No doubt, there will be differences of opinion regarding the interpretation of certain passages. Welcome the learning opportunities involved. Stress the need for dependence on the Holy Spirit to interpret the Scriptures for us. Lead class members to compare various translations and to use the marginal references in their Bibles to locate parallel passages. Encourage research in reference books available in the church library. Seek to lead class members to admit the possible validity of any interpretation which is true to the teaching of the Scriptures as a whole, while each Christian accepts that interpretation which seems to him most clearly to fit the passage in question. Point out that many passages are so rich as to carry several shades of meaning, all of which may be accepted as facets of the message for us.

Audio-Visual Aids

A large map of Palestine is a must for the best teaching of this book. Frequent use of a chalkboard will be effective.

A filmstrip *Matthew's Message* has been prepared for use with this book. It may be shown in its entirety to introduce the study, or it may be used as a summary. Frames may be selected to fit a certain chapter and shown in connection with the presentation of that chapter.

Any of the following filmstrips will furnish other supplementary material. A very effective plan is to introduce a few carefully selected frames or slides at opportune places during the study of a chapter.

The Birth of Jesus (Matt. 2:1–12), 22 frames, color, manual.

Jesus Begins His Galilean Ministry (Matt. 4:13–16), 20 frames, color, manual.

Jesus' First Tour of Galilee (Matt. 8:2–4; 9:1–13), 25 frames, color, manual.

Jesus' Second Tour of Galilee (Matt. 9:18–31), 26 frames, color, manual.

Jesus Withdraws from Galilee (Matt. 15:21–31; 16:13–20), 21 frames, color, manual.

The Last Supper, 28 frames, color, manual.

Jesus' Resurrection, 21 frames, color, manual.

From the list of slides given in the current *Baptist Book Store Catalog,* choose those which relate to incidents presented by Matthew, selecting in particular those slides which fit passages that the author of this textbook stresses. Note in particular slide Cc 670 *Leonardo da Vinci—The Last Supper.* (See p. 129.)

The following motion pictures are available for rental, and may be used as supplementary material. They will be valuable for showing during assembly periods.

Birth of the Saviour, 15 minutes

Jesus and the Fisherman, 15 minutes

Last Journey to Jerusalem, 20 minutes

The Upper Room, 15 minutes

Betrayal in Gethesemane, 15 minutes

Jesus Before the High Priest, 15 minutes

Trial Before Pilate, 15 minutes

The Crucifixion, 20 minutes

The Lord Is Risen, 15 minutes

The foregoing filmstrips, slides, and motion pictures are available at your Baptist Book Store. See the current *Baptist Book Store Catalog* for descriptions and prices.

For Further Reading

The following books offer helpful background material. The listing of a book does not necessarily imply full endorsement of its contents either by the Baptist Sunday School Board or by the author of this text.

Broadus, John A. *Commentary on the Gospel of Matthew*
Davis, William Hersey. *Davis' Notes on Matthew*
Eddleman, H. Leo. *Teachings of Jesus in Matthew 5–7*
Edersheim, Alfred. *Jesus the Messiah*
Ellicott, Charles John. *Matthew*
Erdman, Charles R. *Matthew*
Goodspeed, Edgar J. *Matthew, Apostle and Evangelist*
Morgan, G. Campbell. *Gospel According to Matthew*
Myres, William A. *Design for Happiness*
Stephens, J. Harold. *The Churches and the Kingdom*
Tasker, R. V. G. *Gospel According to St. Matthew*
Thomas, W. H. Griffith. *Outline Studies in the Gospel of Matthew*

For Review and Written Work

Chapter 1

1. Show that the apostle Matthew was well fitted to write the Gospel which appears first in our New Testament.
2. What was Matthew's distinctive purpose in writing his Gospel?

Chapter 2

3. What is the central theme of Matthew's Gospel?
4. What is the place of the church in the kingdom program?
5. Tell something about how the kingdom has been growing.

Chapter 3

6. Mention four or five lessons learned from Matthew's genealogy of Jesus.
7. Tell how Matthew teaches unmistakably that Jesus was born of a virgin.
8. How was the Trinity manifested at the baptism of Jesus?
9. In what three realms of thought did Satan tempt Jesus?

Chapter 4

10. Contrast Christ's plan for attaining happiness with the way the world usually seeks it.
11. What did Jesus mean by "the light of the world" and the "savor" of the salt?
12. Name six areas in which Jesus illustrated the contrast between the old and the new interpretations of the way of righteousness.
13. What are five realms in one's life, implied in the Lord's Prayer, over which Jesus desires to be sovereign?
14. What does it mean to "seek first the kingdom of God and his righteousness"?

Chapter 5

15. Name at least five realms over which Jesus demonstrated his authority and power.
16. Name the twelve apostles.
17. Give some points of warning and encouragement in the in-

145

structions Jesus gave his apostles as he sent them out into Galilee to witness for him.

CHAPTER 6

18. In the parable of the sower and soils, what did each soil represent?
19. Why did the Pharisees hate Jesus?
20. Why was Peter's "great confession" so significant?
21. What is meant by "the keys of the kingdom?" How are they to be used?

CHAPTER 7

22. What did the transfiguration demonstrate, and what did Moses and Elijah represent?
23. What relationships are taught in the two recorded times that Jesus mentioned the church?
24. Discuss briefly the teachings of Jesus about riches and the kingdom.

CHAPTER 8

25. What was the purpose of the triumphal entry into Jerusalem, and what prophecy did it strikingly fulfil?
26. About what three things did the enemies of Jesus seek to ensnare him with captious questions?
27. Give one great teaching about rewards to be learned from the parable of the talents.

CHAPTER 9

28. What is the essential purpose of the Memorial Supper? What are some of the interpretations of it to be avoided?
29. Give your interpretation of Jesus' refusal to sanction violence. Does it relate to going to war to defend one's country?
30. In what ways did Pilate seek to side-step having to make a decision about Jesus?
31. Outline the "alls" in Matthew 28:18–20.
32. What in this study of the Gospel of Matthew has impressed you most? has blessed you most?

NOTES

<u>65</u> PASSAGES OF OLD TESTAMENT
REFERED TO IN MATT.

<u>45</u> PASSAGES OF OLD TESTAMENT
QUOTED IN MATT.

<u>7</u> OF 14 PARABALES IN ONE
CHAPTER

<u>10</u> OF TWENTY MIRACLES IN
ONE CHAPTER